WALES
THROUGH
THE AGES

A CONCISE GUIDE

WALES

THROUGH

THE AGES

A CONCISE GUIDE

By
Martin Miller-Yianni

The Royal Badge of Wales

Copyright and Acknowledgements

Publisher: Martin Miller-Yianni, Yambol, Bulgaria
First Printed Edition 2024

ISBN 978-619-7742-33-6 (paperback)
ISBN 978-619-7742-34-3 (ePub)

A CIP catalogue record for this book is available from:

The National Register of Published Books in Bulgaria
bulevard 'Vasil Levski' 88,
1504 Sofia,
Bulgaria

Title Picture: Welsh Red Dragon
By Soda Sodacan, via Wikimedia Commons

Cover Photograph: Cardiff Castle
By Samuel Meller from Unsplash.com

This book is dedicated to the memory of my music teacher,

Mr. Emlyn Jones.

An accomplished tenor, pianist, and devoted family man with profound humanity, he kindled the musical interests of numerous schoolchildren, irrespective of their varying levels of proficiency.

His energy inspired generations of young individuals to cherish, actively engage in, and cultivate a lasting love for classical music throughout their lives.

Without his influence and guidance, many would traverse life with a musical void.

On a personal note, he forever remains my hero.

By The Author

CONTENTS

"Wales Through the Ages: A Concise Guide" is an engaging and accessible exploration of Welsh history, offering readers a thorough yet approachable overview of the nation's past. Part of a distinguished series on the histories of various countries, this book maintains a high standard of writing, making it an excellent resource for anyone—whether a traveller, tourist, or simply someone keen on deepening their knowledge of Wales.

One of the book's strengths is its ability to recap and explain significant events from previous chapters when necessary. Such recapitulations are inevitable, as the transitions between historical eras often involve overlapping events and key figures. These reminders are not only helpful but essential, ensuring that readers grasp the broader narrative and understand how different periods of Welsh history are interconnected.

Whether you're looking to refresh your memory on a particular era or develop a comprehensive understanding of Wales's past, this book offers dependable information written in British English and serves as an invaluable guide. It invites readers on a captivating journey through time, highlighting the triumphs, challenges, and cultural transformations that have shaped Wales's unique identity.

THE FLAG OF WALES

The flag of Wales, commonly known as the Red Dragon or Y Ddraig Goch, boasts a significant history dating back to the early medieval period. Its design features a red dragon passant on a background of green and white. It wasn't until 1959 that pictured flag of Wales received official recognition.

The connection of the red dragon with Wales can be traced to ancient legends and folklore. The commonly told tale involves a conflict between a red dragon and a white dragon, symbolising the struggle between the Welsh and the invading Saxons. Eventually, the red dragon emerged triumphant, becoming a symbol of Welsh identity and resistance.

The adoption of the red dragon as a symbol of Wales gained prominence during the early 15th century under Owain Glyndŵr, a Welsh prince and rebel leader, who raised the dragon banner in the pursuit of Welsh independence.

In 1485, Henry Tudor, with strong Welsh ties, ascended to the throne as King Henry VII of England after prevailing in the Battle of Bosworth. Henry integrated the red dragon into the Tudor royal arms, further reinforcing its association with Wales.

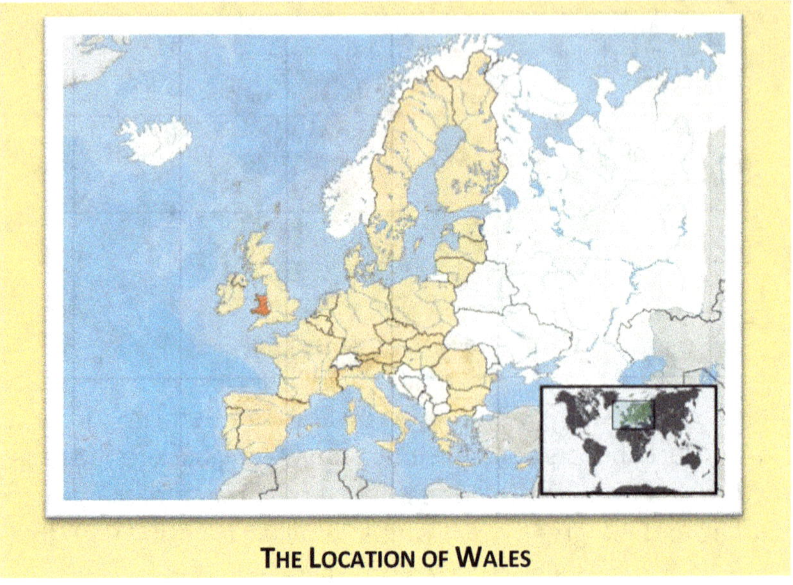

THE LOCATION OF WALES

Wales, part of the United Kingdom, is located to the west of England, sharing its eastern border with its English counterpart. Bounded by the Irish Sea to the north and west, Wales faces the Bristol Channel to the south. Geographically, it showcases diverse landscapes, featuring the central Cambrian Mountains, with the highest peak, Snowdon, reaching 1,085 metres. The River Severn is the longest river in the United Kingdom, originating in Wales.

The country's rich history is evident in its medieval castles, including Conwy, Caernarfon, and Harlech, designated UNESCO World Heritage Sites. The cultural identity of Wales is further highlighted by its official languages, with both English and Welsh (Cymraeg) holding official status. Cardiff, positioned in the south, serves as the capital, while Swansea and Newport are other major cities.

PREHISTORY – C. 43 A.D.

The early history of Wales is shrouded in the mists of prehistory, marked by significant milestones in the Stone Age, Bronze Age, and Iron Age. Archaeological evidence reveals the gradual development of human societies, technological advancements, and cultural practices.

STONE AGE

During the Stone Age in Wales, spanning approximately from 230,000 to 2,000 B.C., our forebears navigated a world vastly different from ours. Although detailed records are absent, archaeological findings offer insights into the lives of these early inhabitants.

In the Paleolithic era, spanning approximately from 230,000 to 12,000 B.C., bands of nomadic hunter-gatherers traversed the expansive landscapes of Wales. During this time, these resilient communities relied on fundamental tools meticulously fashioned from stones, bones, and antlers to fulfil a myriad of tasks, encompassing the intricate arts of hunting and crafting.

As these intrepid groups roamed the land, their survival hinged upon the adept use of rudimentary implements. Stones, shaped into tools for cutting and hunting, served as indispensable assets in their daily pursuits. Bones and antlers, carefully crafted into utensils and weapons, showcased the resourcefulness of these early inhabitants in utilising the available materials.

This era of the Paleolithic not only witnessed the nomadic lifestyle of these hunter-gatherer societies but also highlighted their intimate connection with the environment. The tools crafted from natural elements reflected not only a pragmatic response to survival needs but also the beginnings of human ingenuity and adaptability in the face of the challenges posed by their surroundings.

The Mesolithic period, spanned approximately from 12,000 to 6,000 B.C. The climatic shifts and the ascending sea levels prompted communities in Wales to establish themselves in semi-permanent campsites. This era witnessed a notable adaptation to the evolving environment, with the tools crafted during this time reflecting a heightened level of sophistication in their understanding of the natural surroundings.

A RECONSTRUCTED PRE-HISTORIC SEMI-PERMANENT CAMP

As the climate underwent transformations and sea levels rose, communities strategically chose semi-permanent campsites as their abodes. This decision was driven by a nuanced comprehension of the landscape, as these sites offered a balance between stability and the flexibility required for a nomadic lifestyle. The tools fashioned in the Mesolithic era stand testament to an advanced understanding of the environment, showcasing innovations that facilitated hunting, crafting, and resource utilisation in a more refined manner compared to earlier periods.

This period marked a pivotal juncture where human societies in Wales not only adapted to environmental changes but also showcased a remarkable progression in their ability to interact with and manipulate their surroundings. The Mesolithic era, with its semi-permanent settlements and sophisticated tools, underscores the resilience and ingenuity of the ancient inhabitants as they navigated the challenges posed by a dynamic and ever-changing world.

In the Neolithic era, which roughly covered the period 6,000 to 2,000 B.C., a transformative time unfolded in Wales, heralding a pivotal shift with the introduction of agriculture and the establishment of enduring settlements. This marked a profound departure from the nomadic lifestyle of preceding eras as communities embraced the cultivation of crops and the domestication of animals, ushering in an era of greater stability.

The advent of agriculture in this period signified a monumental leap forward, as communities transitioned from a reliance on hunting and gathering to cultivating their own sustenance. The domestication of animals added another dimension to their burgeoning agrarian lifestyle, contributing to a more reliable and sustainable way of life.

Noteworthy stone monuments became emblematic of this era, with burial chambers and standing stones gracing the landscape for both practical and ceremonial purposes. These imposing structures not only served as markers of significant events and rituals but also reflected the growing complexity of social organisation within these Neolithic communities.

The Lligwy Neolithic Burial Chamber in Moelfre, Anglesey, stands as a notable representation of the era's architectural achievements. This impressive structure, featuring standing stones and burial chambers, becomes a focal point in understanding this time period. Serving practical and ceremonial functions, the Lligwy Burial Chamber is not just an isolated monument but an integral part of the broader picture of Neolithic communities.

The solemn nature of the burial chambers blends with the ceremonial significance of standing stones, creating a harmonious combination that mirrors the intricate social organisation prevalent in these ancient communities. The enduring presence of the Lligwy Neolithic Burial Chamber signifies not only the significance of the events and rituals it hosted but also the lasting impact of these communal practices on the cultural landscape of the time.

As the Moelfre, Anglesey landscape is graced by this monumental structure, it becomes a living representation of the Neolithic era's architectural and cultural progress. The Lligwy Neolithic Burial Chamber, with its steadfast stones and sacred chambers, captures the essence of these times, offering insight into the elaborate makeup of Neolithic life and the enduring heritage it has imprinted on the Welsh landscape.

During this time, structures like longhouses suggested a more complex social organisation. Trade networks likely developed, enabling the exchange of goods and ideas with neighbouring communities. The significance of resources like flint, found in places like Trefil and Penmaenmawr, emphasised their crucial role in tool-making.

LLIGWY BURIAL CHAMBER, MOELFRE, ANGLESEY

The Neolithic era in Wales underscores our ancestors' resilience, marking a pivotal chapter in history. It saw the rise of settled agricultural societies, paving the way for intricate civilisations. During this time, our forebears transitioned from nomadic to stable agricultural communities, defining the era. This laid the groundwork for later civilisations. In Wales, the Neolithic period witnessed the cultivation of crops and animal domestication, fundamentally altering human-environment interaction. This symbiotic relationship laid the basis for sustainable practices, shaping advanced cultures in subsequent ages.

Bronze Age

The Bronze Age, which extended from around 2,000 to 800 B.C. in Wales, we observe notable progress and societal transformations as our predecessors adapted to the changing landscape.

In the Early Bronze Age, spanning roughly from 2,000 to 1,400 B.C., a notable technological advancement unfolded in Wales with the introduction of bronze metallurgy. This period witnessed a significant stride as communities embraced the art of crafting more sophisticated tools, weapons, and ornaments from this alloy, signifying a pivotal shift in their material culture.

The mastery of bronze metallurgy ushered in an era of refined craftsmanship, enabling the creation of implements with enhanced durability and versatility. Tools and weapons fashioned from bronze became emblematic of the technological prowess achieved during this period, reflecting a heightened level of skill and knowledge in metallurgical practices.

Beyond the realm of material advancements, changes in burial practices added another layer to the cultural landscape of the Early Bronze Age. The creation of round barrows and cairns marked a departure from earlier burial customs, suggesting a nuanced evolution in spiritual beliefs and practices. These burial structures not only served as resting places for the departed but also hinted at a growing significance of ritualistic and symbolic elements within the communities of that time.

In Early Bronze Age Welsh burial sites, there is a notable scarcity of weapons in comparison to other artifacts. The absence of evidence pertaining to earlier Bronze Age settlements suggests that farms or hamlets during this period were not fortified.

The Early Bronze Age in Wales, with its embrace of bronze metallurgy and evolving burial practices, stands as a testament to the dynamic interplay between technological progress and cultural shifts during this formative period in history.

From 1,400 to 1,100 B.C., we find ourselves in the times of the Middle Bronze Age, a discernible evolution unfolded in Wales as settlement patterns became more defined. Notable among the landscape were strategic defensive structures such as the Moel-y-Gaer hillfort in North Wales, standing as tangible evidence of a shift towards a more intricate social structure and heightened communal organisation.

MOEL-Y-GAER HILLFORT IN NORTH WALES

The emergence of hillforts like Moel-y-Gaer suggested a deliberate effort to fortify and organise settlements, indicative of a society adapting to new challenges and perhaps reflecting a more complex socio-political landscape. These strategic defensive structures not only provided protection but also underscored the importance of communal collaboration in ensuring the security of the inhabitants.

At the same time, the Middle Bronze Age witnessed a surge in cultural sophistication, exemplified by the production of intricate pottery and metalwork. These artefacts revealed a refined craftsmanship and artistic sensibility, reflecting an increased mastery of materials and techniques. The intricate designs on pottery and the finesse displayed in metalwork spoke volumes about the aesthetic and cultural expressions of the communities during this era.

BRONZE AGE POTTERY FOUND IN CARDIFF

The Middle Bronze Age in Wales stands as a chapter of dynamic change, marked by defined settlement patterns, strategic fortifications, and a flourishing cultural milieu. It serves as a testament to the resilience and adaptability of ancient societies as they navigated the complexities of their evolving environment.

Entering the Late Bronze Age, during the years 1,100 to 800 B.C., witnessed the culmination of significant developments in Wales. Hillforts proliferated across the landscape, underscoring a heightened focus on fortified settlements and the consolidation of social structures. Concurrently, the artistry in metalworking achieved unprecedented levels, reflecting a pinnacle of craftsmanship and creative expression.

The proliferation of hillforts during this era suggested a strategic expansion of fortified sites, indicating not only a commitment to defence but also a reflection of evolving socio-political dynamics. These hillforts served as both protective strongholds and symbols of community identity, contributing to the shaping of a landscape marked by fortified prominence.

The mark of metalworking artistry became a hallmark of the Late Bronze Age, with craftsmen achieving new heights in the intricacy and sophistication of their creations. The artifacts produced during this period not only served functional purposes but also testified to a cultural flourishing, showcasing a mastery of metallurgical techniques and an appreciation for aesthetic finesse.

Trade networks expanded significantly during this time, connecting Wales with distant regions, as revealed by the discovery of exotic items in archaeological sites. This influx of foreign goods underscored the integration of Wales into broader networks of exchange, suggesting a heightened level of interaction and interconnectedness with neighbouring cultures. Improved communication and transportation likely played a pivotal role in facilitating these connections, allowing for the exchange of ideas, materials, and goods that enriched the developing culture of the Late Bronze Age in Wales.

Despite the absence of written records, the archaeological findings portray a society in flux during the Bronze Age in Wales. The mastery of metallurgy, the construction of fortified sites, and the flourishing of cultural expressions collectively contribute to the intricate historical fabric of this era.

IRON AGE

In the Iron Age in Wales, covering approximately 800 B.C. to 43 A.D., we witness a continuous process of societal development and cultural changes as communities adapt to the demands of the time.

Entering the Early Iron Age, spanning roughly from 800 to 400 B.C., witnessed a gradual transition from bronze to iron metallurgy in Wales. This pivotal shift in metalworking techniques brought forth the creation of more durable tools and weapons, signifying a transformative phase in technological evolution.

As iron supplanted bronze, the production of tools and weapons experienced a notable enhancement in durability and functionality. Iron, with its intrinsic strength, became the material of choice, contributing to the development of implements that were not only robust but also more versatile in meeting the evolving needs of ancient communities.

Hillforts, exemplified by structures like Tre'r Ceiri in North Wales, gained prominence during this era as defensive strongholds. The ascendancy of such fortifications pointed towards an increasingly intricate social structure, where fortified settlements played a pivotal role not only in defence but also in asserting territorial control and fostering communal cohesion.

Burial practices underwent discernible changes in the Early Iron Age, marked by evidence of both inhumation and cremation. This shift in funerary customs suggested a nuanced evolution in spiritual beliefs and societal rituals, reflecting a complex interplay between cultural, religious, and social dynamics within these ancient communities.

The Early Iron Age in Wales emerges as a period of dynamic transformation, where technological advancements, fortified landscapes, and evolving burial practices collectively contribute to the multifaceted network of ancient societal development.

Advancing into the Middle Iron Age, spanning approximately from 400 to 100 B.C., witnessed a pronounced trend in Wales as settlements fortified themselves, underscoring a growing imperative for security and territorial control. Simultaneously, advancements in ironworking propelled the production of intricate artifacts and tools, showcasing a continued refinement in metallurgical skills and craftsmanship.

Settlements during this period exhibited a heightened emphasis on fortification, suggesting a response to an evolving geopolitical landscape. The strategic fortification of these sites became emblematic of a society navigating challenges and seeking to safeguard its interests. These fortified settlements not only served defensive purposes but also played a role in shaping the socio-political dynamics of the time.

The Middle Iron Age marked a continued progression in ironworking, leading to the creation of intricate artifacts and tools. The mastery of iron as a medium facilitated the production of implements that were not only functional but also aesthetically sophisticated. This period witnessed a flourishing of material culture, with artifacts reflecting the technical prowess and artistic sensibilities of the communities.

Tribal societies in Wales became more distinct during the Middle Iron Age, contributing to a rich and diverse cultural milieu. These distinct tribal identities added layers of complexity to the social fabric, fostering unique traditions, beliefs, and practices within different communities. The interactions and exchanges between these tribal societies enriched the cultural landscape of the era, shaping the multifaceted identity of ancient Wales.

In the Late Iron Age, spanning from around 100 B.C. to 43 A.D., Wales experienced notable progress. Striking hillforts, exemplified by structures like Castell Henllys in Pembrokeshire, showcased a sophisticated approach to defensive architecture and a keen understanding of strategic considerations within the society.

CASTELL HENLLYS HILLFORT IN PEMBROKESHIRE

Increased engagement in trade became apparent during this era, as demonstrated by the unearthing of Roman artifacts. This archaeological evidence in Wales highlights an active participation in broader trade networks, indicating its connection to extensive routes and economic interactions. The presence of Roman artifacts suggests a dynamic interplay between the indigenous Iron Age cultures of Wales and the expanding influence of the Roman Empire.

The Late Iron Age also witnessed the emergence of a distinctive artistic style in pottery and metalwork, reflecting a unique cultural identity. Skilled artisans demonstrated notable creativity, incorporating intricate designs into their creations that mirrored the aesthetic preferences and cultural subtleties of the period. These artistic expressions serve as tangible indicators of the flourishing creativity within the communities of the Late Iron Age.

Despite the absence of written records, archaeological findings provide valuable insights into the dynamic societies of Iron Age Wales. The mastery of iron metallurgy, the strategic construction of hillforts, and the crafting of intricate artifacts collectively contribute to the captivating historical tale of Wales during this time.

SUMMARY

In the prehistoric era of Wales, extending until approximately 43 A.D., the land was home to diverse Celtic tribes and native groups. These communities practised agriculture, raised animals, and developed unique material expressions. Hillforts were prevalent across the landscape, reflecting organised societies and defensive measures. Megalithic structures such as burial chambers and standing stones were erected, revealing the inhabitants' ritual customs and spiritual beliefs. This period set the stage for the region's cultural legacy, and its course shifted notably with the arrival of the Romans in 43 A.D., signifying a pivotal moment in Welsh history.

PEOPLE:

Early Settlers (Mesolithic and Neolithic): Nomadic hunter-gatherer communities who gradually transitioned to settled life, engaging in early agriculture.

Beaker People (Early Bronze Age): Introduced distinctive pottery and were associated with the early use of bronze in Wales.

Hillfort Builders (Late Bronze Age and Iron Age): Communities constructing impressive hillforts for defensive and strategic purposes, reflecting advanced social organisation.

PLACES:

Paviland Cave: Known for the "Red Lady of Paviland," a Paleolithic burial site providing insights into early ceremonial practices.

Bryn Celli Ddu: A Neolithic burial mound on Anglesey, possibly associated with rituals and celestial observations.

Trefael Stone Circle: A well-preserved stone circle from the Bronze Age, reflecting ceremonial and ritual significance.

Tre'r Ceiri: A prominent Iron Age hillfort in North Wales, showcasing advanced defensive structures and societal organisation.

Mesolithic Transition: The shift from nomadic hunter-gatherer lifestyles to settled communities engaged in agriculture during the Neolithic.

Introduction of Bronze Metallurgy: Signalled technological advancement during the Early Bronze Age, transforming tool and weapon production.

Construction of Hillforts: Prominent during the Late Bronze Age and Iron Age, these fortified settlements indicate strategic planning and societal complexity.

Roman Interaction: During the Late Iron Age, Wales experienced increased contact with the Roman Empire, leading to cultural exchange and adaptation.

Cultural Flourishing: Evident in the development of unique pottery styles, intricate metalwork, and the construction of impressive structures during various prehistoric periods.

C. 43 – 410 A.D.

Around the year 43 A.D., the Romans initiated their conquest of Wales, marking a significant chapter in the region's history. Led by Governor Gaius Suetonius Paulinus, Roman forces faced resistance from local tribes, most notably the Silures. The Silures, known for their fierce opposition to Roman rule, put up a determined fight against the advancing Roman legions.

ROMAN CONQUEST AND ESTABLISHMENT

The initial stages of the Roman conquest involved strategic military campaigns to subdue resistant tribes and establish control over key territories. As Roman legions advanced through Wales, they encountered diverse landscapes, from rugged terrains to dense forests, presenting both challenges and opportunities for tactical maneuvers.

The Romans employed advanced military techniques and engineering skills to overcome natural obstacles and the defensive strategies of the native population. The construction of temporary camps and fortifications facilitated the consolidation of Roman control in conquered areas. These early military outposts laid the groundwork for the later establishment of more permanent Roman forts.

An eminent site that emerged during the period 1,400 and 1,100 B.C. is Segontium, situated in the contemporary region of Caernarfon. Segontium played a pivotal role as a crucial Roman fort, strategically positioned to exert control over the surrounding regions and uphold order in the recently conquered territory. The establishment of such forts stands as a resounding testament to the formidable military prowess and organisational efficiency of the Roman forces during this period.

Segontium's location in present-day Caernarfon was not arbitrary; rather, it was a calculated strategic choice. Positioned strategically, the fort served as a linchpin in the Roman effort to assert dominance and manage the newly acquired territories. This strategic placement allowed the Romans to exercise control over key transportation routes, facilitating communication and logistical support across the region.

The construction of Segontium exemplified the Roman commitment to military excellence. The fort's architectural design showcased not only structural ingenuity but also a meticulous consideration of defensive capabilities. With walls, watchtowers, and other defensive features, Segontium stood as an imposing symbol of Roman military might, deterring potential challenges to their authority.

Beyond its military function, Segontium played a crucial role in fostering Roman influence and cultural integration. The fort served as a hub for administrative activities, contributing to the Romanisation of the local populace. The presence of Roman soldiers and officials in Segontium left an indelible mark on the social and cultural landscape, influencing the daily lives of the inhabitants and contributing to the amalgamation of Roman and local traditions.

In essence, Segontium, with its strategic significance, not only reflected the military prowess of the Roman forces but also underscored their ability to arrange and administer newly conquered territories. This fortified stronghold stands as a historical testament to the intricate interplay between military strategy, organisational efficiency, and cultural influence during a pivotal period in Welsh history.

The resistance from the Silures and other local tribes necessitated a combination of military strength, diplomacy, and cultural assimilation by the Romans. The clash of cultures and the imposition of Roman authority began shaping the trajectory of Wales during this period, leaving a lasting impact on the socio-political and cultural landscape.

The events of 43 A.D. set the stage for a prolonged period of Roman influence, characterised by the establishment of forts, roads, and the gradual integration of Wales into the broader Roman administrative and cultural framework. This conquest would shape the trajectory of Wales for centuries to come, marking the beginning of an era that would see the fusion of Roman and indigenous Welsh elements.

2ND CENTURY ISCA AUGUSTA ROMAN FORTRESS

In the illustrious 2nd century, Isca Augusta, gracefully positioned in the present-day Caerleon, ascended to eminence as a pivotal Roman fortress within the bounds of Welsh history. Originally conceived as a bastion for Roman legions, Isca Augusta transcended its martial roots, blossoming into a dynamic settlement replete with the grandeur of an amphitheatre and the indulgence of baths. This fortified enclave not only stood as a formidable military redoubt but also developed into a vibrant epicentre of commerce, governance, and cultural convergence, contributing profoundly to the intricate mosaic of Roman influence making its way through the makeup of Welsh identity.

Concurrently, amid the same time, the sagacious Romans embarked upon monumental feats of infrastructure in the Welsh realm, with the construction of nothing short of arteries coursing through the land – the venerable Sarn Helen and the resplendent Fosse Way. Sarn Helen, gracefully navigating the undulating Welsh terrain, bore testament to the ingenuity of Roman engineering, whilst Fosse Way, a majestic thoroughfare, artfully linked Exeter to the northern Lincoln, charting a course through the verdant expanses of Wales.

SARN HELEN NAVIGATING THE UNDULATING WELSH TERRAIN

These meticulously crafted conduits not only expedited seamless communication, facilitated the flow of trade, and orchestrated the strategic ballet of Roman legions but also etched an indelible mark upon the Welsh tableau, shaping its cultural, economic, and historical panorama with the grandeur befitting an era of imperial splendour.

THE AGE OF ROMAN INFLUENCE AND TRIALS

As the 3rd century unfolded, the profound impact of Romanisation unfurled across the cultural canvas of Wales. This transformative era witnessed the infusion of Latin, reshaping the linguistic fabric of Welsh communication with a distinct Roman resonance. The adoption of Latin not only altered spoken discourse but also left an indelible mark on the linguistic legacy of Wales.

Simultaneously, a revival in architectural pursuits unfolded, giving rise to structures influenced by Roman aesthetics as symbols of wealth. These buildings, embellished with imposing columns, graceful arches, and meticulously crafted mosaics, stood as tangible expressions of Roman magnificence. However, it was the intricately designed mosaics adorning these constructions that brought an added layer of artistic sophistication to this period.

The mosaics discovered from this era not only showcased exceptional artisanship but also conveyed captivating narratives engraved in stone. These mosaic floors, adorned with elaborate patterns and vivid depictions, demonstrated a seamless integration of local Welsh influences with the refined design principles of Roman architecture. Each mosaic recounted a visual story, portraying a blend of cultural elements and a pursuit of aesthetic excellence.

Far from being mere decorative elements, these mosaic artworks served as a form of expression that spoke volumes about the cultural exchange between the indigenous Welsh communities and the Roman inhabitants. Depicting scenes of daily life, mythological themes, and intricate geometric designs, the mosaic floors embodied a fusion of artistic traditions. The artistry of the mosaics emerged as a dynamic expression of the convergence of two distinct cultural identities.

Furthermore, the structures adorned with these mosaics became communal spaces, providing inhabitants with settings where they could gather amidst the artistic splendour. As individuals traversed these mosaic-decorated floors, they not only walked on beautifully arranged stones but also experienced a shared cultural narrative woven through the combination of Roman refinement and Welsh heritage.

Mosaics from this era stand as noteworthy artifacts, enriching the architectural panorama with their artistic brilliance and encapsulating a distinctive chapter in the history of cultural amalgamation. The mosaic floors, with their detailed craftsmanship and vibrant compositions, serve as eloquent witnesses to a time when Roman influence seamlessly blended with indigenous Welsh sensibilities, leaving behind an artistic legacy that transcended the boundaries of both cultures.

However, amidst this cultural renaissance, challenges emerged. External threats necessitated the strengthening of Roman frontiers and the strategic fortification of military outposts across Wales. The delicate balance between Roman influence and local autonomy underwent scrutiny, revealing the nuanced interplay between conquerors and the resilient spirit of the conquered.

AN EXAMPLE OF ROMAN MOSAIC FOUND IN CAERLEON

Wales in the 3rd century signifies a captivating era where the recalls of Romanisation resonated through linguistic corridors and architectural landscapes. This amalgamation of diverse elements etched a chapter of cultural synthesis, defining an episode marked not only by the magnificence of Roman influence but also by the unwavering resilience of the Welsh spirit, steadfastly navigating external pressures.

WALES FACES EXTERNAL THREATS, AND ROMANS FORTIFY FRONTIERS

In the latter part of the 3rd century, Wales grappled with external threats, prompting a strategic response from the

Romans. Faced with the spectre of potential invasions, the Romans embarked on a significant effort to fortify their frontiers, marking a crucial phase in the ongoing interaction between Wales and the Roman Empire.

During this period of heightened vulnerability, Wales became a focal point for external pressures, prompting the Romans to fortify key strategic positions. The systematic reinforcement involved the construction of robust defensive structures, including walls, watchtowers, and other installations. These defensive measures not only underscored the strategic importance of Wales within the Roman Empire but also showcased the adaptability and resilience of Roman military strategies in the face of evolving geopolitical challenges.

This time signifies a complex interplay of geopolitical factors, where external threats triggered a proactive response from the Romans, leading to the fortification of frontiers. This period reflects the ongoing dynamic between imperial control imperatives and the persistent challenges posed by external forces, shaping the historical trajectory of Wales during this era.

DECLINE AND WITHDRAWAL

In the early 4th century, Wales found itself entangled in the intricate challenges of an economic and political downturn, mirroring the struggles of the vast expanse of the Roman Empire. The once-thriving pillars of economic prosperity and political stability within Welsh territories began to show signs of strain, reflecting the systemic issues echoing across the Roman realm. This period witnessed a confluence of factors contributing to the decline, including economic stressors, political instability, and the gradual erosion of the once-pervasive influence of the Roman administrative apparatus. The tangible impacts of these challenges permeated Wales, ushering in a shift in the socio-political landscape and setting the stage for subsequent phases of historical evolution.

As the early 5th century dawned, the tenuous grip of Roman authority over Wales began to unravel in the face of formidable challenges. The once-mighty Roman forces, grappling with internal strife and external pressures on an unprecedented scale, reached a critical juncture. This marked the initiation of a momentous decision – the strategic withdrawal of Roman forces from the territories that constituted Wales. Key figures such as Roman commanders and local leaders played pivotal roles in shaping the course of events during this tumultuous period.

One notable figure associated with this era is Flavius Stilicho, a prominent general and statesman of Vandal descent who served as a high-ranking officer in the Roman army. Stilicho was influential in Roman politics during the late 4th and early 5th centuries, and his decisions and strategies had an impact on the Roman military's movements in various regions.

The commonly cited traditional end date for this monumental event is 410 A.D., encapsulating the culmination of the Roman retreat from Welsh lands. This withdrawal heralded a transformative chapter, signifying the conclusion of Roman dominion and heralding a new era for Wales. Notable places such as Caerleon and Deva, which had once been vital Roman strongholds, now stood witness to the changing tides of history.

The vacuum left by the departing Romans created a void that would be filled by emergent socio-political dynamics, with influential figures like local chieftains and tribal leaders stepping into leadership roles. These figures played a crucial part in shaping the evolving moments of Wales during this pivotal time.

ROMAN GENERAL FLAVIUS STILICHO

This momentous withdrawal resonated through thc corridors of time, leaving an indelible mark on the historical story of Wales. It laid the groundwork for the unique cultural and political landscape that would emerge in the centuries to come. The departure of Roman forces became a defining episode, with individuals and locations playing key roles in the unfolding chapters of Welsh history, profoundly influencing the trajectory of the nation.

SUMMARY

During the Roman era in Wales the landscape underwent significant changes under Roman dominion. Upon their arrival in 43 A.D., the Romans established settlements, roads, and fortifications, assimilating Wales into the larger Roman Empire. Urban centres like Caerleon emerged as focal points, showcasing Roman architectural styles and administrative practices. The Welsh populace encountered novel technologies, trade opportunities, and cultural exchanges through their interactions with the Romans. Despite these transformative elements, challenges arose, exemplified by the resistance spearheaded by figures like Caratacus. These times in Welsh history left an enduring imprint, shaping societal structures, infrastructure, and cultural assimilation within the broader Roman context.

PEOPLE:

Caratacus (Caradog): A prominent leader of the Catuvellauni tribe, who resisted the Roman invasion in the early stages.

Boudica: Queen of the Iceni tribe in eastern Britain, known for leading a major uprising against Roman rule in 60-61 A.D.

Gnaeus Julius Agricola: Roman governor who conducted military campaigns in Wales, consolidating Roman control and implementing Romanisation policies.

PLACES:

Segontium (Caernarfon): A significant Roman fort and settlement in northwest Wales, serving as a key military and administrative centre.

Deva Victrix (Chester): A Roman fortress near the Welsh border, influencing the dynamics of the region.

Moridunum (Carmarthen): A Roman town in southwestern Wales, becoming an urban centre and hub of Roman influence. Venta Silurum (Caerwent): An important Roman town showcasing Roman urban planning and infrastructure.

EVENTS:

Roman Conquest (43–78 A.D.): The period during which Wales was gradually incorporated into Roman Britain through military campaigns.

Roman Campaigns in Wales (late 1st century): Led by governors like Ostorius Scapula and Quintus Veranius, these campaigns aimed to subdue resistance and solidify Roman control.

Boudica's Revolt (60–61 A.D.): A major uprising led by Queen Boudica against Roman rule in southeastern Britain, impacting the broader context of Roman Britain.

Construction of Roman Roads (1st–4th centuries): Including the notable Sarn Helen, facilitating communication, trade, and Roman influence across Wales.

End of Roman Rule (410 A.D.): With the decline of the Roman Empire, Wales experienced the withdrawal of Roman forces, marking the end of direct Roman governance.

410 A.D. – 1093 A.D.

As Roman influence waned, Wales entered a dynamic phase of transition. Native kingdoms emerged, facing external threats such as Viking raids and the subsequent Norman Conquest, which left a lasting impact on the political landscape.

DECLINE OF ROMAN INFLUENCE AND THE RISE OF NATIVE KINGDOMS

In the Sub-Roman era of Welsh history, spanning from around 410 to 600 A.D., a notable transition unfolded as Roman influence diminished, giving rise to indigenous kingdoms. This period, marked by a complex interweaving of historical events, migrations, and cultural shifts, presented a nuanced story.

The departure of Roman legions circa 410 A.D. created a vacuum, empowering local communities in Wales to declare their independence. The absence of a central authority led to the fragmentation of the region into smaller, self-governing entities, exacerbated by the breakdown of Roman infrastructure.

External challenges, including raids by Irish and Germanic tribes like the Anglo-Saxons, tested Welsh communities, prompting them to adapt and fortify against external threats.

Indigenous leaders emerged in response to these challenges, consolidating power and establishing their own kingdoms. Remnants of Roman urban centres, such as Caerleon and Caernarfon, continued to shape the evolving socio-political landscape, and Welsh elites, now regional leaders, worked to maintain stability.

Vortigern, a significant figure in Welsh history, is often associated with the tumultuous period during the 5th century. His reign is intertwined with the decline of Roman influence in Britain and the subsequent influx of various Germanic tribes. While historical accounts of Vortigern's life are somewhat scarce and often blurred with mythology, his role in the transitional phase of Britain remains a subject of interest.

Vortigern is said to have been a British ruler, possibly a king or warlord, who emerged as a central figure during the post-Roman era. The period was marked by the withdrawal of Roman legions from Britain, leaving a power vacuum that led to internal strife and external threats from invading forces.

One of the most notable aspects of Vortigern's reign is his alleged role in inviting the Saxon mercenaries, led by Hengist and Horsa, to Britain to help defend against Pictish and Scottish raids. However, the alliance took an unexpected turn as the Saxons, allegedly dissatisfied with their rewards, turned against the Britons, leading to increased conflicts.

According to the legendary accounts, Vortigern is famously associated with constructing a fortress on Mount Snowdon in

North Wales known as Dinas Emrys. The construction of this fortress is linked to a legend involving a red and a white dragon, representing the conflict between the Welsh and the invading Saxons. The tale suggests that Vortigern sought to build a stronghold but faced challenges as the foundations repeatedly collapsed. The wizard Merlin, in this tale, is said to have attributed the instability to a struggle between the two dragons beneath the ground.

AN ARTIST'S ENGRAVING OF DINAS EMRYS

Vortigern's story is also connected to the legendary figure of Ambrosius Aurelianus, who is sometimes considered a historical basis for King Arthur. The accounts are often interwoven with folklore and mythical elements, making it challenging to discern the precise historical details of Vortigern's reign.

While Vortigern's rule is shrouded in both history and legend, his significance lies in being a key figure during a critical juncture in Britain's history. The complexities of the post-Roman era, the interaction with various tribal groups, and the attempts to navigate the challenges of the time make Vortigern a compelling and enigmatic character in the story of Wales.

VORTIGERN AND THE RED AND A WHITE DRAGONS

The spread of Christianity marked a profound cultural shift in the Sub-Roman period, with missionaries like Saint Patrick and Saint David playing pivotal roles in the conversion of the Welsh to Christianity. This religious transformation not only influenced spiritual beliefs but also contributed to the development of a distinct Welsh identity.

The Sub-Roman period laid the groundwork for medieval history in Wales, witnessing the rise of early Welsh kingdoms, the blending of native and incoming cultures, and the enduring impact of Christianity. These pivotal centuries played a crucial role in shaping the historical trajectory of Wales.

NORSE INVASIONS ALONG THE COAST

The tumultuous period spanning the 8th to the 10th centuries in Wales witnessed formidable Viking raids, where Norse seafarers executed audacious invasions along the Welsh coast, leaving a lasting impact on the region. This era, marked by a clash of cultures, involved key figures such as King Offa and notable locations, including Offa's Dyke.

KING OFFA STATUE AT TINTERN TRAIN STATION

The Vikings, renowned for their seafaring skills, exploited the vulnerability of coastal settlements, instilling fear in Welsh communities with their swift longships. These raids were strategic campaigns aimed at acquiring wealth, resources, and new territories.

The Norse incursions wrought havoc along the Welsh coastline, pillaging villages and ransacking monasteries. Notably, the raid on the monastery of Llanddwyn saw Vikings desecrating sacred spaces and seizing valuable treasures, echoing through generations as a symbol of audacious brutality.

Despite being subjected to external threats, the Welsh, led by local rulers like King Offa, took proactive measures. Offa, known for his efforts to strengthen the Mercian kingdom, played a crucial role in fortifying coastal defences. Offa's Dyke, a monumental earthwork, served as a significant defensive structure, stretching across the border between Mercia and Wales.

Amidst the chaos, tales of heroic resistance emerged, with Welsh leaders rallying against the Viking incursions. These accounts, though possibly embellished, testified to the indomitable spirit of the Welsh people. King Offa's strategic prowess and the construction of Offa's Dyke added layers to the defence against the Viking raids.

Despite the strife caused by the Viking incursions, cultural exchanges occurred. The adversarial encounters between the Norse and the Welsh, coupled with interactions with figures like King Offa, facilitated a cross-pollination of ideas, technologies, and traditions, contributing to the evolving identity of Wales.

The Viking raids from the 8th to the 10th centuries, stand as a pivotal chapter in Welsh history. The scars left by these incursions became part of Welsh collective memory, shaping the region's resilience, cultural development, and enduring spirit in the face of formidable challenges.

MAP OF THE OFFA'S DYKE ROUTE

NORMAN INCURSIONS AND THE ESTABLISHMENT OF MARCHER

The historical period spanning 1066 to 1093 in Wales was profoundly shaped by the Norman Conquest, a complex time characterised by Norman incursions and the establishment of Marcher Lordships. This era unfolded as a multifaceted network, rich in intrigue, conflict, and the recalibration of power dynamics, with key individuals, significant locations, and pivotal events playing crucial roles in shaping Welsh history.

The impetus for the Norman Conquest was the Battle of Hastings in 1066, where William the Conqueror's victory not only secured his claim to the English throne but also had far-reaching consequences for Wales. Norman forces, eager to extend their influence, ventured across the Welsh border.

A noteworthy outcome of the Norman Conquest was the inception of Marcher Lordships, a distinct political and military system along the England-Wales border. Marcher Lords, appointed by the English crown, enjoyed considerable autonomy, acting as both a deterrent against potential Welsh resistance and instruments of Norman authority.

The Norman forays into Wales during this period were marked by a strategic combination of military campaigns and the erection of formidable fortifications. The landscape of Wales became punctuated with imposing castles, emblematic structures that not only served as defensive bastions but also stood as powerful symbols of Norman strength and dominance.

Chepstow Castle, situated on the banks of the River Wye, exemplified the Norman approach to fortress construction. Built in the late 11th century, Chepstow Castle boasted an imposing curtain wall, a towering great tower, and strategically positioned gatehouses. The castle's strategic location near the border with England underscored its significance in controlling key routes and maintaining Norman influence in the region. Chepstow Castle, with its commanding presence, became a formidable stronghold projecting Norman authority deep into Welsh territories.

CHEPSTOW CASTLE, MONMOUTHSHIRE

Pembroke Castle, another prominent example, was strategically positioned along the southwestern coastline of Wales. Its construction in the early 12th century transformed the local landscape, as the imposing stone structure overlooked the Milford Haven waterway. Pembroke Castle's design showcased the military sophistication of the Normans, featuring a massive keep, a fortified gatehouse, and a strategic layout that maximised defensive capabilities. The castle's strategic location not only secured Norman territorial claims but also facilitated maritime control, further solidifying Norman dominance in the region.

These castles served dual purposes as defensive structures and symbols of Norman supremacy. The architectural grandeur and military prowess displayed in the construction of these fortifications conveyed a clear message of Norman dominance to the local Welsh population. The imposing nature of these castles not only deterred potential adversaries but also functioned as administrative centres, enabling the Normans to exert control over the newly acquired territories.

PEMBROKE CASTLE, PEMBROKESHIRE

These Norman fortifications left an enduring mark on the Welsh landscape. These structures, with their strategic locations and architectural magnificence, served as tangible manifestations of Norman military might and played a crucial role in shaping the power dynamics during this era of historical flux.

Gruffudd ap Cynan, a prominent figure among indigenous Welsh rulers, emerged as a stalwart leader in the arduous struggle against the encroaching Norman expansion. His valiant efforts, marked by tales of courageous battles and strategic alliances, played a pivotal role in shaping the enduring narrative of Welsh resistance during this tumultuous period.

Gruffudd's leadership was characterised by a series of determined military campaigns aimed at repelling Norman advances into Welsh territories. His prowess on the battlefield became legendary, and his strategic acumen in forming alliances with other Welsh leaders further strengthened the collective resistance against the Norman forces.

However, Gruffudd's resilience was not without its trials. At one point in his tumultuous journey, he found himself imprisoned. The reasons behind his incarceration were multifaceted. Political intricacies and internal conflicts within Wales, coupled with external pressures from Norman adversaries, led to moments of discord among Welsh rulers. Gruffudd, in the course of navigating these complex dynamics, faced political challenges that eventually resulted in his imprisonment.

During his time in captivity, Gruffudd's spirit remained unbroken. His imprisonment, rather than serving as a defeat, became a testament to his enduring commitment to the cause of Welsh independence. The challenges he faced behind bars only fuelled the flames of resistance within him.

Upon regaining his freedom, Gruffudd continued his unwavering efforts against the Norman expansion. His leadership became even more crucial as he navigated the intricate web of Welsh politics, forging alliances and consolidating support for the collective cause. Gruffudd's ability to overcome adversity, both on and off the battlefield, contributed significantly to the resilience of Welsh resistance during this tumultuous era.

In the broader context of Welsh history, Gruffudd ap Cynan stands as a symbol of indomitable spirit and steadfast determination. His efforts, entwined with tales of bravery, imprisonment, and strategic manoeuvres, form an integral part of the enduring story of Welsh resistance against the Norman expansion during this challenging period.

GRUFFUDD AP CYNAN BEING FREED FROM IMPRISONMENT BY THE NORMAN LORD HUGH D'AVRANCHES IN CHESTER

The encounter between Norman and Welsh cultures resulted in a nuanced fusion of traditions, languages, and governance systems. The Marcher Lordships, ostensibly under English control, became arenas where Norman lords interacted with the Welsh population, fostering a dynamic exchange of ideas and practices.

The Norman Conquest's enduring impact on Wales is evident in the altered political landscape marked by the establishment of Marcher Lordships. This transformative period laid the foundation for centuries of cultural exchange, conflict, and coexistence along the borderlands between England and Wales.

In contemplation, the Norman Conquest of Wales from 1066 to 1093 stands as a pivotal chapter, intricately shaping the socio-political landscape and cultural evolution of the region. The legacy of this period persists in the majestic castles that grace the Welsh countryside and in the intricate makeup of Welsh history, where the influence of the Normans intertwines with the resilient spirit of the Welsh people.

SUMMARY

In the period following the Roman era, Wales entered a dynamic phase characterised by a blend of local developments and external influences. As Roman forces withdrew around 410 A.D., Wales underwent a transition towards regional self-governance. This era saw the rise of distinctive Welsh kingdoms and the preservation of Celtic traditions. The influx of Anglo-Saxons and later Viking interactions introduced both cooperation and conflicts, shaping the political landscape. Figures like King Arthur gained prominence in Welsh mythology during this time. The establishment of early Christian monasteries and the fusion of Celtic and Christian beliefs added a layer of cultural richness. The post-Roman era laid the foundation for the medieval period, establishing the backdrop for the challenges and accomplishments that would unfold in Wales in the ensuing centuries.

PEOPLE:

Saint David (Dewi Sant): A prominent figure in Welsh Christianity, St. David is the patron saint of Wales. He is believed to have lived during the 6th century and played a crucial role in the spread of Christianity in Wales.

Hywel Dda (Hywel the Good): A 10th-century ruler of Wales, Hywel Dda is known for his codification of Welsh laws, creating a legal system that influenced Welsh governance for centuries.

Gruffudd ap Cynan: A key figure during the 11th century, Gruffudd ap Cynan was a King of Gwynedd who played a significant role in the struggles for power and control in Wales.

PLACES:

St. David's Cathedral: Founded in the 6th century near the birthplace of St. David, this cathedral became a major centre of pilgrimage and an important religious site.

Tintern Abbey: Though the original abbey was founded in 1131, the site has significance in this period. The Cistercian abbey in Monmouthshire played a crucial role in the medieval Welsh monastic landscape.

Dinas Powys: A hillfort located near Cardiff, Dinas Powys is an archaeological site that provides insights into early medieval settlements in Wales.

EVENTS:

Battle of Badon: Believed to have taken place around 516 A.D., the Battle of Badon is often associated with King Arthur and is considered a significant event in the defence of Britain against invading forces.

Viking Raids: During the late 8th and early 9th centuries, Wales experienced Viking raids and invasions, which had a profound impact on the region's history.

Norman Conquest of Wales: The Normans, under William the Conqueror, began their incursions into Wales in the late 11th century. This period laid the groundwork for later conflicts and the integration of Norman influence in Wales.

1093 – 1485

The medieval period in Wales witnessed a complex interplay of Norman rule, Welsh resistance, and involvement in the Wars of the Roses. It was a time of shifting allegiances, cultural resilience, and the struggle for autonomy.

GRADUAL INCORPORATION INTO THE KINGDOM OF ENGLAND

Between the years 1093 and 1282, Wales found itself entwined in a captivating saga of Norman rule and conquest, a tale that intricately shaped its gradual integration into the fabric of the Kingdom of England. This protracted period, marked by a flux of power dynamics, nuanced cultural exchanges, and territorial reshaping, etched an enduring account into the archives of Welsh history.

The Normans wielded their influence through the strategic expansion of Marcher Lordships, accompanied by the calculated erection of castles strategically strewn across the Welsh topography. Monuments to Norman authority, exemplified by the likes of Conwy and Caernarfon, not only asserted dominance but also served as formidable military strongholds, leaving an indelible mark on the architectural makeup of Wales.

The reign of King Henry II witnessed a determined drive to assert English supremacy over Wales, employing military campaigns to subjugate Welsh rulers and seamlessly integrate their domains into the English fold. Figures such as Owain Gwynedd responded with a nuanced blend of resistance and diplomacy, deftly navigating the intricate web of relationships with the English crown.

In the 13th century, the sagacious Llywelyn the Great orchestrated a skillful consolidation of power, safeguarding Welsh autonomy through diplomatic finesse. The Treaty of Montgomery in 1267 formally acknowledged Welsh sovereignty, establishing a transient equilibrium in the complex interplay between Wales and England.

However, this fragile equilibrium was violently disrupted in subsequent decades. The ambitious endeavours of Edward I culminated in the forceful conquest of Wales, characterised by relentless military campaigns and the construction of imposing Edwardian fortresses, including the monumental Caernarfon and Harlech. The Statute of Rhuddlan in 1284 formalised the incorporation of Welsh territories into the English legal and administrative framework, heralding a profound transformation in the socio-political fabric of Wales.

The once-autonomous Welsh Princes, notable figures such as Owain Gwynedd and Llywelyn the Great, found themselves relegated to subjects within the Kingdom of England. The imposition of English law and governance aimed to erode Welsh cultural distinctiveness, ushering in a more comprehensive assimilation of Wales into the English state.

The period spanning from 1093 to 1282 marks another pivotal transformation for Wales. The Norman conquest, amid its inevitable conflicts, facilitated intricate cultural exchanges that indelibly shaped the contours of Welsh identity. The eventual annexation into the Kingdom of England signified the denouement of an era, with the enduring presence of castles acting as tangible, monumental reminders of the intricacies and complexities of this transformative chapter in Welsh history.

LLYWELYN THE GREAT

48

UPRISINGS AGAINST ENGLISH RULE

The 13th century in Wales unfolded, revealing the tumultuous and captivating Welsh Wars of Independence. This elaborate series of uprisings against English rule painted a vivid portrait of Welsh identity and resilience, a historical canvas infused with tales of unwavering defiance, charismatic leaders, and the poignant collision of cultures. It stands as a testament to the indomitable spirit coursing through the veins of the Welsh people.

The genesis of these conflicts finds its roots in Edward I's calculated conquest of Wales in the latter part of the 13th century. The annexation of Welsh territories and the imposition of English governance planted the seeds of discontent, sparking widespread unrest among the Welsh population. Stripped of their autonomy, the Welsh Princes emerged as central figures in a dramatic theatre of dissent and opposition.

In 1277, King Edward I took a decisive step in asserting English dominance by declaring Llywelyn ap Gruffydd a rebel, marking the onset of the First War of Welsh Independence. The English forces, strategically mobilised, initiated a series of military campaigns that proved pivotal in reshaping the political landscape of Wales.

English armies, advancing from Carmarthen, achieved success by defeating the princes of Deheubarth, consolidating control over this southern Welsh territory. Simultaneously, forces from Chester overwhelmed Powys Fadog, and armies from Shrewsbury executed a successful campaign to retake Maelienydd, Builth, Brycheiniog, and Gwrtheyrnion.

The culmination of these military successes led to the Treaty of Aberconwy, a significant turning point in Welsh history. Under the terms of this treaty, Edward I compelled Llywelyn to cede control of the entirety of Wales, excluding only Gwynedd west of the River Conwy. The once-unified realms of Powys Fadog and Deheubarth were dismantled, further consolidating English authority over Welsh territories.

In 1282, the complex dynamics took an unexpected turn when Dafydd ap Gruffudd, Llywelyn's younger brother, previously perceived to be in collaboration with King Edward I, coordinated a rebellion against the English forces. This marked a significant internal shift in Welsh politics, as Dafydd's rebellion drew Llywelyn into the conflict, reshaping the landscape of Welsh resistance.

The ensuing conflict witnessed a fierce struggle for independence, with Dafydd and Llywelyn leading a determined resistance against the English forces. The rebellion underscored the intricate alliances and rivalries within Welsh noble families and their relationships with the English crown.

Ultimately, the rebellion against England in 1282 left an enduring impact on the course of Welsh history. Llywelyn's involvement, driven by a desire for Welsh autonomy, added a layer of complexity to the conflict. The events of this period not only shaped the political boundaries of Wales but also laid the foundation for subsequent struggles for Welsh independence.

The latter stages of the conflict witnessed an unstoppable surge in the construction of Edwardian castles, including the grandiose structures of Caernarfon and Conwy. These imposing fortifications stood as formidable symbols of English supremacy, casting shadows over the Welsh landscape. Dafydd ap Gruffudd's capture in 1283 marked the dramatic denouement of organised resistance, culminating in his execution and the formal annexation of Wales into the Kingdom of England.

The Welsh Wars of Independence transcended mere military struggles, causing cultural conflicts. The Welsh language and traditions faced relentless suppression, with deliberate efforts to impose English customs aiming to erode the distinct Welsh identity. Yet, even in the face of adversity, the Welsh resiliently preserved their proud cultural heritage, by their resistance against English rule.

The legacy of the Welsh Wars of Independence resonates deeply in the annals of Welsh history. The tales of Llywelyn the Last, Dafydd ap Gruffudd, and the indomitable Welsh populace enduring hardships to safeguard their identity reverberate through the ages. The scars of these wars are palpable in the landscape, where the grand Edwardian castles stand as silent witnesses to a poignant period of struggle and determination, shaping the enduring spirit of Wales in the most dramatic and embellished hues.

WELSH INVOLVEMENT IN THE DYNASTIC CONFLICT

The Wars of the Roses, spanning the tumultuous years from 1455 to 1485, stand as dynastic conflicts between the venerable houses of Lancaster and York, vying for the coveted mantle of the English throne. Within this sweeping account, Wales emerges as a veritable feast of fluctuating loyalties, epic battles, and the rise of indomitable Welsh figures who left an indelible mark on history.

The Welsh implication in the Wars of the Roses unfolds against the backdrop of complex family ties intertwining Welsh and English noble houses. The Tudors, the Herberts, and the

Vaughans, illustrious Welsh families, find themselves entangled in the intricate political dance, with the Tudors ultimately assuming a pivotal role as the conflict unfurls.

In the embryonic stages of the Wars, Welsh nobility, like characters in a dramatic play, align themselves with either the House of Lancaster or the House of York, driven by familial bonds, regional affinities, or Machiavellian political considerations. The hallowed grounds of Wales bear witness to significant clashes, including the 1461 Battle of Mortimer's Cross and the climactic 1485 Battle of Bosworth, where Welsh valour shapes the destiny of nations.

The Battle of Mortimer's Cross in 1461, a pivotal engagement during the Wars and had notable repercussions in Wales, adding a layer of complexity to the regional dynamics. The conflict unfolded between Lancastrians loyal to King Henry VI and Yorkists led by Edward, later known as Edward IV, whose victory held profound implications for both England and Wales. The battlefield near the River Lugg in Herefordshire saw Edward IV's forces securing a decisive win, strengthening his claim to the English throne.

This triumph extended its influence into Wales as Edward IV sought to assert control over the Welsh territories. The battle's aftermath contributed to the shaping of Welsh allegiance during this tumultuous period, as the ascendancy of the Yorkists impacted the political landscape and alliances within Wales, further intertwining the fates of the two realms. The Battle of Mortimer's Cross, therefore, played a crucial role in not only determining the course of English history but also influencing the dynamics and loyalties within Wales during the Wars of the Roses.

Jasper Tudor, a luminous figure in this medieval saga and uncle to the future Henry VII, emerges as the orchestrator of Welsh destiny. A staunch Lancastrian, Jasper conducts strategic military campaigns within the Welsh heartlands, rallying support for the Lancastrian cause. Despite facing formidable challenges, his efforts illuminate the strategic platform of Wales in the grand theatre of the Wars of the Roses.

BATTLE-OF-MORTIMERS-CROSS (1461)

The Tudor connection to Wales achieves its peak with the rise of Henry Tudor, the prodigious scion born within the hallowed walls of Pembroke Castle. Returning from exile in Brittany, Henry stages a theatrical bid for the English throne, setting the stage for the climactic denouement at the Battle of Bosworth in 1485. Here, amid the rolling Welsh hills, Henry's triumph over Richard III heralds the establishment of the Tudor dynasty, casting a spell that echoes through time.

The accession of Henry VII marks not merely the end of the Wars of the Roses but heralds the dawn of a new horizon for Wales. His reign, akin to a soothing melody after a storm, brings stability, and the Tudor dynasty etches its name into the chronicles of both English and Welsh history.

In the grand event of the Wars of the Roses, where Welsh involvement is vital thread, we witness the intricate ballet of familial, regional, and political forces. The battles fought on Welsh soil, the conflicts within its borders, and the ascent of the Tudors illustrate the complex togetherness that directs this chapter of history. The enduring legacy of the Wars of the Roses resonates, shaping the political destiny of England and Wales for generations to come.

SUMMARY

In the medieval era, a complex compound of political, social, and cultural developments unfolded. This period witnessed the consolidation of Welsh principalities and ongoing interactions with the English Crown. The Norman Conquest of Wales in the late 11th century resulted in the establishment of Marcher lordships, significantly influencing Welsh governance. Notable Welsh leaders, including Owain Glyndŵr, played pivotal roles in resisting English dominance. The Wars of the Roses in the 15th century added further intricacies to the political landscape. This era marked a flourishing of Welsh literature, especially poetry, with figures like Dafydd ap Gwilym making noteworthy contributions.

PEOPLE:

Llywelyn the Great (Llywelyn Fawr): A powerful Welsh prince, Llywelyn ap Iorwerth, known as Llywelyn the Great, played a key role in consolidating and unifying Welsh territories during the 12th and 13th centuries.

Owain Glyndŵr: A charismatic and rebellious figure, Owain Glyndŵr led the Welsh Revolt against English rule in the early 15th century. He briefly established a Welsh parliament and was a symbol of Welsh resistance.

Henry VII (Harri Tudur): Born in Pembroke Castle, Henry VII became the first monarch of the Tudor dynasty and played a pivotal role in the Wars of the Roses, ending the conflict with his victory at the Battle of Bosworth in 1485.

PLACES:

Conwy Castle: Built by Edward I in the late 13th century as part of his conquest of Wales, Conwy Castle is a well-preserved fortress and a UNESCO World Heritage Site.

Harlech Castle: Another of Edward I's castles, Harlech Castle played a strategic role during the Wars of the Roses and the Glyndŵr Rising.

Tretower Court and Castle: Located in Powys, Tretower is an impressive medieval manor and castle that reflects the social structure and architecture of the time.

Edward I's Conquest of Wales (1277-1283): Edward I launched military campaigns to conquer Wales, constructing numerous castles to exert control and influence over the Welsh territories.

Owain Glyndŵr's Revolt (1400-1415): Owain Glyndŵr's rebellion aimed at asserting Welsh independence and resisting English rule. Although ultimately unsuccessful, it left a lasting impact on Welsh identity.

Wars of the Roses (1455-1487): A series of civil wars between the rival houses of Lancaster and York for control of the English throne. The final battle, the Battle of Bosworth, resulted in Henry Tudor's ascent to the throne as Henry VII.

1485 – 1707

The Tudor and Stuart periods marked significant political and social transformations. From the Tudor dynasty's influence to the events of the Civil War and the Restoration, Wales experienced a series of changes that would shape its future.

HENRY VII, HENRY VIII, AND THE ACTS OF UNION WITH ENGLAND

The Tudor period, spanning from 1485 to 1603, unfolded as a magnificent and profound transformation for Wales under the reigns of Henry VII and Henry VIII. This period witnessed a togetherness of political, cultural, and social shifts, exemplified by the enactment of the Acts of Union with England, which left an enduring imprint on Welsh history.

Henry VII, the inaugural sovereign of the Tudor dynasty, ascended to the throne with the victory in the Battle of Bosworth in 1485. Hailing from Pembroke Castle in Wales, Henry sought to reconcile the houses of Lancaster and York through marriage to Elizabeth of York. His reign aimed to bring stability to England and Wales post the Wars of the Roses.

Beneath Henry VII's rule, Wales experienced a period of relative peace and some autonomy. The Acts of Union (1536 and 1543), or the Laws in Wales Acts, were enacted during his reign, intending to integrate Wales more closely into the Kingdom of England. They replaced the traditional Welsh legal system with English common law and restructured Wales into shires for improved administration.

HENRY VII BORN IN PEMBROKE CASTLE

Henry VIII, the son of Henry VII, continued his father's policies in Wales while asserting English authority. Despite concerns about the potential loss of Welsh identity, the Acts of Union contributed to administrative efficiency and enhanced economic ties between Wales and England.

Culturally, the Tudor Period in Wales saw a resurgence of the Welsh language and literature. The translation of the Bible into Welsh, known as the "Bishop's Bible," by William Salesbury and Richard Davies played a crucial role in preserving Welsh language and fostering cultural resilience.

Religious changes during the Tudor Period, particularly the English Reformation, had significant impacts on Wales. The dissolution of monasteries under Henry VIII led to the loss of cultural and religious centres, affecting Welsh communities. The spread of Protestantism, however, left a lasting mark on Welsh religious practices.

In the latter part of the Tudor Period, Elizabeth I's reign played a crucial role in bringing about increased stability in Wales. The Tudor monarchy's ongoing efforts to consolidate power and ensure order persisted during this time, fostering conditions conducive to economic growth and cultural advancement in Wales.

Elizabeth I pursued political measures to further integrate Wales into the broader English domain. The Acts of Union in 1536 and 1543, initiated by her predecessors and continued under her rule, sought administrative and legal uniformity, eliminating distinct Welsh laws and assimilating Wales into the English legal system. This political alignment aimed to centralise authority, diminish regional autonomy, and promote a sense of unity.

Economically, stability was nurtured by promoting trade and commerce. Tudor monarchs, including Elizabeth I, recognised the economic potential of Wales, investing in industries like mining and agriculture to stimulate growth. Efforts to curb border lawlessness and piracy also enhanced the security of trade routes, supporting economic activities.

Culturally, stability was established by encouraging the use of the English language and fostering education. The Tudor monarchy actively endorsed the dissemination of English language and culture in Wales, contributing to a more unified national identity. The establishment of grammar schools and the promotion of literacy facilitated cultural development, enabling the Welsh population to engage with broader intellectual and artistic trends.

Elizabeth I's adept political strategies, diplomatic skills, and effective management of religious tensions further contributed to an overall sense of stability. Her ability to navigate the complexities of the time, including challenges posed by the Protestant Reformation, played a key role in maintaining order and creating an environment in which economic and cultural pursuits could thrive.

The achievement of stability in Wales during the later Tudor Period, particularly under Elizabeth I, was a multifaceted process. It encompassed political integration, economic growth, and cultural advancement, all working together to foster a more unified and prosperous Welsh society within the broader Tudor English framework.

The Tudor Period in Wales struck a delicate balance between integration and the preservation of Welsh identity. While the Acts of Union aimed at administrative unification, the Tudor monarchs, recognising the importance of Welsh loyalty, allowed for a measure of cultural autonomy. This era laid the groundwork for subsequent developments in Wales, shaping its political, cultural, and linguistic landscape for generations.

ELIZABETH I BROUGHT STABILITY TO WALES

CIVIL WAR, COMMONWEALTH, AND THE RESTORATION

The captivating period known as the Stuart Period, spanning from 1603 to 1707, unfolded as a riveting episode in Welsh times gone by, intricately entwined with the complex events of the English Civil War, the interregnum of the Commonwealth, and the subsequent Restoration. Beyond being a mere chronicle of political upheaval, this period emerged as a welding of transformative occurrences, leaving an enduring imprint on the very essence of Wales.

In the initial years of the Stuart Period, under the reigns of James I and Charles I, the surface appeared serene. However, beneath this facade simmered a cauldron of discontent fuelled by issues such as religious freedoms, the limits of royal authority, and the pursuit of equitable parliamentary representation. Within Wales, the aspiring Welsh gentry and elite sought to assert their influence within the broader political landscape, reflecting the nuanced layers of societal aspirations.

The Battle of Edgehill, which unfolded on 23rd October 1642 during the English Civil War, held considerable significance for Wales. As Royalist and Parliamentarian forces clashed near the town of Kineton in Warwickshire, the repercussions of this pivotal engagement reverberated deeply across Welsh soil.

In this confrontation, the Royalist army, led by King Charles I, contested the Parliamentarian forces commanded by the Earl of Essex. The undulating terrain of Edgehill posed challenges for both sides, resulting in a fierce and inconclusive battle. While lacking a clear victor, the consequences of Edgehill were far-reaching, setting the stage for the protracted conflict that unfolded during the English Civil War.

For Wales, the aftermath of Edgehill marked the beginning of a transformative period. The struggle between Royalists and Parliamentarians had direct implications for Welsh society, contributing to shifts in social, political, and religious dynamics. The battles, including Edgehill, played a role in shaping the destiny of Wales within the broader context of the English Civil War.

The multifaceted nature of societal changes witnessed during this period reflected the impact of the conflict on Welsh soil. The battles, were not merely distant events but had a tangible and lasting influence on the fabric of Welsh life. As the English Civil War unfolded, Wales underwent a metamorphosis that left an indelible mark on its social and religious landscape.

The ultimate outcome saw the Parliamentarians triumph, ushering in the establishment of the Commonwealth under the formidable leadership of Oliver Cromwell. This transformative period bore witness to a metamorphosis in the social and religious fabric of Wales, reflecting the multifaceted nature of societal changes.

The Stuart Restoration in 1660, marked by the triumphant return of Charles II, brought about a nuanced shift in the political landscape. Wales, mirroring the broader English panorama, witnessed the splendid reinstatement of the monarchy and the Church of England. A deliberate effort ensued to intricately integrate Wales into the English legal and administrative framework. The Clarendon Code, a legislative opus of its own, aimed to enforce ecclesiastical conformity, casting a shadow over dissenting groups within Wales and illuminating the intricate dance between centralisation and regional autonomy.

The later years of the Stuart Period in Wales were characterised by a crescendo of heightened political and religious tensions, setting the stage for the grandeur of the Glorious Revolution of 1688. The accession of William III and Mary II heralded an era of constitutional monarchy and Protestant supremacy, demonstrating the enduring impact of international and national events on the regional dynamics of Wales. The subsequent Act of Union with England in 1707 marked a formal fusion, solidifying the union of England and Wales under the banner of the Kingdom of Great Britain, thereby embedding Wales even further into the grand foundations of the emergent British state.

THE EVE OF THE BATTLE OF EDGEHILL (1642)

The Stuart Period in Wales emerged as a captivating throng, not just of political and religious transformations, but as a rich and nuanced cultural landscape. The legacies forged during this time laid a profound foundation for evolution within Wales with the ever-shifting dynamics of the British state, underscoring the resilience and adaptability of the Welsh spirit amidst the tumultuous currents of history.

ACT OF UNION WITH ENGLAND IN 1707

SUMMARY

In the early modern period Wales underwent significant transformations in political, social, and cultural realms. The Tudor era marked the assimilation of Wales into the Kingdom of England through the enactment of the Laws in Wales Acts, diminishing certain aspects of its distinct governance. Religious changes during the Reformation also had a lasting impact on Welsh society. While the Welsh language faced challenges, it endured as a crucial cultural element. The Stuart period brought further changes, with the English Civil War affecting Wales and the subsequent establishment of the Commonwealth. The Act of Union in 1707 formalized the union between England and Wales. This period witnessed a dynamic interplay of adaptation and preservation, shaping Wales' course within the broader context of early modern Britain.

PEOPLE:

Henry VIII: The second monarch of the Tudor dynasty, Henry VIII, played a crucial role in the English Reformation, which had implications for Wales. His dissolution of the monasteries significantly altered the religious landscape.

Thomas Cromwell: A chief minister to Henry VIII, Thomas Cromwell was instrumental in the dissolution of the monasteries and the restructuring of religious institutions in England and Wales.

Henry VII (Harri Tudur): Although previously mentioned, Henry VII's reign (1485-1509) is significant for the establishment of the Tudor dynasty, marking the end of the Wars of the Roses.

PLACES:

Plas Mawr: Located in Conwy, Plas Mawr is an exceptionally well-preserved Elizabethan townhouse, offering insights into the architecture and lifestyle of the late 16th century.

St. Fagans National Museum of History: Situated near Cardiff, St. Fagans is an open-air museum showcasing Welsh history and culture, with reconstructed buildings from different historical periods.

EVENTS:

Acts of Union (1536-1543): The Laws in Wales Acts of 1536 and 1543 were crucial legislative acts that incorporated Wales into the Kingdom of England, creating the legal entity now known as England and Wales.

English Civil War (1642-1651): Wales experienced the effects of the English Civil War, with battles and conflicts between Royalists and Parliamentarians. Some castles, like Raglan, played roles in the conflict.

Glorious Revolution (1688): The Glorious Revolution had implications for Wales as it influenced the political landscape in England and marked the beginning of constitutional changes.

1707 – 1800

The 18th century ushered in the Industrial Revolution, bringing about radical economic and social shifts. Wales became a crucible for industrial innovation, with coal mining and manufacturing driving urbanisation and societal changes.

GROWTH OF COAL MINING, IRON INDUSTRY, AND URBANISATION

The grand Industrial Revolution, gathering momentum from the mid-18th century onwards, unfurled a spellbinding and transformative chapter in the history of Wales, etching an indelible tale across its verdant landscapes and societal contours. This epochal period witnessed an extraordinary confluence of forces, as the relentless expansion of coal mining, the flourishing iron industry, and the tidal wave of urbanisation cascaded through the Welsh terrain.

Wales, blessed with bountiful coal reserves, assumed a role of paramount importance in the nascent coal Cendustry, with the coal-rich enclave of South Wales standing as a crucible of industrial progress. The exploitation of these coal resources emerged as the lifeblood propelling the wheels of industrialisation, with coal metamorphosing into a precious fuel source, animating the rhythmic pulse of steam engines, the intricate machinations within factories, and the locomotives that traversed the newfound arteries of progress.

The South Wales Coalfield, ensconced amid the embrace of rich anthracite and bituminous coal veins, ascended to regal prominence as a major theatre for coal mining production. Towns such as Merthyr Tydfil and Aberdare witnessed an astonishing development, as collieries proliferated, animated by the revolutionary advent of steam-powered pumps that performed the miraculous extraction of coal from hitherto unfathomable depths.

The serendipitous union of coal and iron ore in the Welsh crucible played an important role in nurturing the burgeoning iron industry. In locales such as Merthyr Tydfil, under the stewardship of luminaries like Richard Crawshay and Anthony Bacon, ironworks attained eminence for their grand scale and operational efficiency. The blast furnaces, stoked by the black gold of Welsh coal, spewed forth copious quantities of iron, a vital elixir for the construction of machinery, the sinuous arteries of railways, and the sinewy sinews of nascent infrastructure.

Wales, positioned as a crucial centre for iron production, played a vital role in supplying iron products to the expanding British market during the Industrial Revolution. This contribution was pivotal in driving the successful surge of this transformative era. Within Wales, the Pontcysyllte Aqueduct, a testament to engineering brilliance conceived by the visionary Thomas Telford in the early 19th century, holds particular significance. It stands as a symbol not only of innovative infrastructure but also of ingenuity in harnessing its resources for industrial progress of Wales.

Thomas Telford, a distinguished engineer born in Scotland in 1757, became a prominent figure in Britain's industrial landscape. His vision and expertise left an enduring impact, with the Pontcysyllte Aqueduct serving as a prime example of his engineering prowess.

Completed in 1805, this aqueduct spans the River Dee in Wrexham, North Wales, utilising significant amounts of Welsh iron in its construction. The aqueduct's remarkable design features a cast iron trough supported by 18 slender stone pillars, showcasing the rich resources and engineering capabilities of Wales. Standing at a height of 38 meters and stretching over a length of 307 meters, it facilitated the efficient transport of canal boats across the river.

The Pontcysyllte Aqueduct holds profound significance for Wales, representing not just an engineering achievement but a testament to the nation's vital role in the Industrial Revolution. Its construction highlighted the innovative use of Welsh iron and underscored the importance of local resources in driving industrial progress. In essence, the aqueduct stands as a proud symbol of the contribution by Wales to the industrial transformation that shaped the nation's history.

The industrialisation of Wales unfurled as a panorama of unprecedented urban growth, where towns and cities expanded with a rapidity that mirrored the fervor of the Industrial Revolution. Merthyr Tydfil, transcending its origins as a modest market town, blossomed into a bustling industrial metropolis, emblematic of the breathtaking urbanisation that defined this transformative era.

However, this whirlwind of urbanisation brought forth its own set of challenges. The surge of eager workers outpaced the capacity of housing and infrastructure, giving rise to the hurried construction of terraced houses that now stand as poignant relics of the societal transformation from rustic agricultural life to the bustling dynamism of industrial urban existence.

THE PONTCYSYLLTE AQUEDUCT

Yet, amidst the economic prosperity bestowed by the Industrial Revolution, Wales grappled with profound social challenges. Workers in mines and factories toiled under arduous conditions, enduring protracted hours, scant remuneration, and precarious safety measures. The expanding Chartist movement, gaining momentum in the industrialised enclaves of Wales, bore witness to the impassioned quest for political and social reforms, a resonant echo of the collective yearning for an amelioration of living and working conditions.

The Industrial Revolution in Wales stands as an intriguing wealth of growth, innovation, and societal metamorphosis. The convergence of coal mining, the iron industry, and urbanisation thrust Wales into the heart of industrial development sweeping across its landscape and culture. The remnants of collieries, ironworks, and urban infrastructure stand as poignant and tangible relics, bearing witness to the pivotal role Wales had in the industrial transformation that unfolded during the resplendent times of the 18th and 19th centuries.

ENCLOSURE ACTS, POPULATION GROWTH, AND EMERGING INDUSTRIAL SOCIETY

The 18th century in Wales unfolded as a period marked by profound societal changes, intricately shaped by the confluence of the Enclosure Acts, a burgeoning population, and the emergence of an industrial society. These influential forces not only rewrote the tale of Welsh life but left an enduring imprint on landscapes, communities, and the very fabric of societal identity.

The implementation of the Enclosure Acts during this era cast a substantial shadow over the traditional agricultural scenery. Communal lands, once the heart of community life, underwent a drastic transformation as these legislative measures privatised and enclosed open fields. The consequences reverberated through rural existence, accentuating disparities between wealthier landowners and smaller farmers who found themselves displaced. This legislative shift not only altered physical landscapes but also triggered societal disruptions and dislocations.

In parallel, the 18th century witnessed a notable demographic surge in Wales. The convergence of improved agricultural practices and advancements in public health led to an unprecedented population increase. Larger families became more prevalent, sparking a discernible demographic expansion that reshaped the rhythms of Welsh life. The familiar cadence of agrarian existence gave way to a population seeking new horizons and economic opportunities.

Against this backdrop of change, the advent of an industrial society marked a pivotal moment. Traditional agrarian landscapes underwent a change in evolution into vibrant urban centres, fundamentally redefining Welsh identity. Towns and cities transformed into hubs of industry, drawing a workforce eager for opportunities in burgeoning sectors. This shift from rural to urban living not only redefined societal demographics but also reshaped cultural norms, laying the groundwork for a new social order.

HUB OF INDUSTRY IN NANT Y GLO, MONMOUTHSHIRE

Amidst these transformations, notable figures played integral roles. The architects of the Enclosure Acts, wielding legislative power, shaped the contours of landownership and community life. Influential landowners, such as those involved in the enclosure process, left an indelible mark on the socio-economic structure of Wales.

However, the path towards industrialisation presented its own set of challenges. The rapid construction of factory housing mirrored cramped and often substandard living conditions for the burgeoning working class. The emergence of this new social stratum represented a departure from age-old farming traditions and set the stage for the formation of labour movements advocating for the rights and welfare of the industrial workforce.

The 18th century in Wales encapsulated a dynamic and intricate era of social evolution, sculpted by the interplay of legislative changes, demographic shifts, and the onset of industrialisation. These multifaceted threads, persist in shaping the socio-economic and cultural dynamics that continue to define Wales in the present day.

SUMMARY

In the 18th century Wales experienced a period of profound historical transitions across various domains. The Acts of Union in 1707 officially united England and Wales under a single political entity. Industrialisation began to impact Wales, particularly in mining and metallurgy, contributing to economic changes and urbanisation. The century also witnessed the rise of nonconformist religious movements, shaping the religious landscape. Social and political reforms gained momentum, with figures like Thomas Pennant contributing to a burgeoning interest in Welsh history and culture. The 18th century in Wales was characterised by a complex interplay of economic shifts, religious developments, and cultural awakenings that laid the groundwork for future societal transformations.

PEOPLE:

Robert Walpole: Often considered the first Prime Minister of Great Britain, Robert Walpole's political influence extended into Wales, marking the early stages of the Hanoverian era.

Thomas Pennant: A Welsh naturalist and travel writer, Thomas Pennant's works, including "A Tour in Wales," contributed to the documentation of Welsh landscapes, culture, and natural history during the 18th century.

Griffith Jones: A clergyman and educationalist, Griffith Jones played a significant role in promoting literacy and education in Wales through the circulating schools and the Welsh Charity School movement.

PLACES:

Tredegar House: Located near Newport, Tredegar House is a grand mansion that played a role in Welsh social and political life during the 18th century, hosting influential figures and events.

Powis Castle: A medieval castle turned country house, Powis Castle in Welshpool reflects the architectural and cultural transitions of the period.

EVENTS:

Acts of Union (1707 and 1800): The Acts of Union with England and Scotland in 1707 and with Ireland in 1800 had implications for Wales, as it was administratively united with England under the Kingdom of Great Britain.

Industrial Revolution: Wales experienced the transformative effects of the Industrial Revolution during the 18th century, particularly in areas such as coal mining and iron production. The growth of industries impacted the socio-economic landscape.

78

Methodist Revival: The 18th century saw the emergence of the Methodist movement, with figures like John Wesley and George Whitefield, which had a significant impact on religious life in Wales, fostering a spiritual revival.

1800 – 1901

The 19th century continued the trajectory of industrialisation, with Wales playing a pivotal role in the coal and iron industries. Concurrently, social reforms, population growth, and cultural developments laid the groundwork for modern Welsh identity.

CONTINUED INDUSTRIALISATION, EXPANSION OF RAILWAYS, AND SOCIAL REFORMS

The Victorian Era, spanning from 1837 to 1901, unfolded as a resplendent and transformative chapter in the Welsh chronicle. Against the grandiose backdrop of Queen Victoria's reign, a sound of change echoed through the valleys and hills, orchestrated by the unyielding surge of industrialisation, the intricate expansion of railways, and the profound chords of social reform. This era etched an indelible masterpiece of Welsh society, intricately making changes that redefined its economic panorama, connectivity, and social intricacies.

The rhythmic heartbeat of industrialisation, a continuous drumroll echoing from preceding centuries, resonated with newfound vigour in Victorian Wales. Coal mining and iron industries, deeply embedded as stalwarts of the nation's economic edifice, experienced an unprecedented growth. The South Wales Coalfield, a formidable contributor, ascended to a central role, providing the essential fuel that stoked the fervent furnaces of progress.

RAILWAY STATION IN NEYLAND, WALES

In the iron-rich landscapes of Merthyr Tydfil and Dowlais, the fervent glow of industrial prowess brilliantly illuminated the skyline. Ironworks thrived, forging substantial quantities of the versatile metal pivotal for construction, shipbuilding, and the burgeoning railway sector. The once tranquil and pastoral panorama underwent a captivating change, factories and chimneys punctuating the valleys like soaring spires, a testament to the indomitable spirit of human ingenuity.

The Victorian Era bore witness to the burgeoning growth of an intricate labyrinth of railways, sinuously connecting the diverse

Welsh terrain. These iron arteries, coursing across valleys and hills with serpentine grace, intricately linked industrial hubs, ports, and urban centres. They emerged as vital conduits, not merely facilitating the seamless movement of raw materials, goods, and people, but serving as the very arteries that sustained the pulse of industries propelling the Welsh economic engine.

Among the extraordinary feats of British engineering were the Conwy Railway Bridge, a breathtaking marvel that defied the laws of gravity, and the strategic expansion of the Vale of Neath Railway. These railway projects went beyond their economic significance, heralding a paradigm shift in travel, fostering enhanced connectivity, and promoting mobility within Wales while extending its reach far beyond its borders.

The Conwy Railway Bridge, designed by Robert Stephenson and completed in 1848, is an iconic structure spanning the Conwy River in North Wales. This tubular bridge is an engineering masterpiece, employing innovative techniques to support the railway tracks within a hollow iron tube. Its construction marked a pioneering achievement in Victorian engineering, facilitating efficient rail travel across challenging terrains.

The strategic expansion of the Vale of Neath Railway, particularly during the 19th century, Wales played a crucial role in transportation landscape. This railway network connected the industrial heartlands of South Wales, facilitating the transportation of coal and iron to the ports for export. It not only stimulated economic growth but also transformed the region's accessibility and connectivity.

These railway projects brought about a profound transformation in Wales. They provided not only economic benefits but also facilitated cultural exchange and strengthened social ties by improving accessibility to different parts of the country. Notwithstanding, the Conwy Railway Bridge and the expansion of the Vale of Neath Railway became enduring symbols of Welsh industrial and engineering prowess, shaping its history and contributing to the broader narrative of Britain's industrial revolution.

THE CONWY RAILWAY BRIDGE

The Victorian Era unfolded as a chapter resonating with calls for social justice, workers' rights, and educational progress. Figures like Robert Owen, an influential social reformer, stood as towering pillars of change, ardently championing cooperative societies and improved working conditions. The establishment of the Taff Vale Railway Workers' Union in 1872 marked a watershed moment, a clarion call in the struggle for workers' rights that reverberated across industries.

Simultaneously, the spirit of reform permeated the realm of education, symbolised by the Welsh Intermediate Education Act of 1889. This legislative landmark sought to dismantle barriers to education, striving to provide accessible and quality learning opportunities for the burgeoning Welsh population.

Beyond the resounding clank of machinery and the sprawling network of railways, the Victorian Era witnessed a stirring resurgence of pride in Welsh culture and identity. The beginning of the Eisteddfod tradition, a vibrant celebration of Welsh literature, music, and performance, emerged as a cultural beacon. It fostered a profound sense of national pride, nurturing the preservation and promotion of the Welsh language and heritage amidst the tumultuous currents of industrialisation.

In essence, the Victorian Era in Wales unfolded as a distinct change for Wales. The relentless march of industrialisation, the sinuous network of railways, social reforms, and a cultural renaissance intricately shaped the landscape, economy, and identity of Wales during this transformative period. The sounds of the Victorian Era resonate in the very soul of Wales, eternally woven into its rich history and heritage.

WALES BECOMES A MAJOR COAL-PRODUCING REGION.

The 19th century in Wales unfurled as a dazzling times of industrial progress resonating through its verdant valleys, catapulting the nation into an unrivalled hub in the global coal mining industry. Against the ceaseless hum of machinery and the rhythmic chorus of pickaxes, Wales ascended as a pivotal player in the coal production domain during this transformative era.

Coal, once latent in the geological embrace of the Welsh landscape, underwent a majestic turnaround into the pulsating force propelling an expanding industrial empire. This century witnessed an unprecedented surge in coal mining activities, notably in the South Wales Coalfield, celebrated for its opulent coal seams that fuelled the insatiable appetites of industrialisation.

The valleys, including the transformative landscapes of Merthyr Tydfil, Rhondda, and the Rhymney Valley, underwent profound metamorphoses, transforming into vibrant hubs of industry. Collieries adorned the panorama, each strike of the pickaxe and the sounds of machinery contributing acts of progress. Extracted from the depths, coal emerged as the quintessential energy source propelling steam engines, locomotives, and the sprawling machinery that defined the period.

The newfound eminence in Wales as a major coal-producing region transcended local boundaries; its impact resonated on the global stage. Welsh coal emerged into a coveted resource internationally, propelling the engines of progress for nations navigating the vast seas of industrialisation. Its significance extended from steamships charting distant oceans to the burgeoning railway networks, playing an indispensable role in shaping global industrial advancements.

Beyond the industrial theatre, coal mines intricately wove themselves into Welsh communities. Towns and villages burgeoned around collieries, cultivating a symbiotic relationship between industry and society. The rows of miners' cottages nestled in the hills bore witness to the human impact of coal mining—a resilient community forged in the crucible of labour, navigating both the triumphs and tribulations.

The ascent of Wales as a major coal-producing region was not without its trials. The unforgiving conditions within the mines, the inherent dangers faced by miners, and the unrelenting demands of labour painted a stark and poignant reality. Yet, amidst these challenges, there were triumphs—testaments to the indomitable spirit and camaraderie of the mining communities that persisted in the face of adversity.

MAP OF COALFIELDS IN WALES (19TH CENTURY)

The 19th century in Wales unfolded as a resplendent chapter, where the subterranean wealth of coal became the driving force behind industrial prowess. The coal mines, with their labour wading through time, not only fuelled the furnaces of industry but also etched a profound and enduring legacy in the annals of global industrialisation. Today, the valleys and hills stand as witnesses to this legacy, where the remnants of coal dust tell the captivating tale of Wales as a major coal-producing region.

SUMMARY

In the 19th century Wales underwent significant changes that influenced its socio-economic, political, and cultural fabric. The Industrial Revolution brought about notable shifts, with the expansion of coal mining, iron and steel industries, and the development of urban centres. Social and political transformations, such as the Chartist movement advocating for political reforms, marked this era. The revival of Welsh language literature, led by figures like Saunders Lewis, played a pivotal role in preserving cultural identity. Additionally, the establishment of the National Eisteddfod contributed to the promotion and celebration of Welsh arts and traditions. The 19th century in Wales was characterised by a dynamic interplay of industrialisation, political activism, and cultural revival, laying the foundation for the ongoing evolution of the region.

PEOPLE:

David Lloyd George: A prominent Welsh politician, David Lloyd George played a significant role in British politics during the late 19th and early 20th centuries. He served as the Prime Minister of the United Kingdom during World War I.

Thomas Telford: A Scottish civil engineer with extensive contributions in Wales, Thomas Telford was involved in the construction of the Pontcysyllte Aqueduct and other infrastructure projects.

Lady Llanover (Augusta Hall): A patron of Welsh culture, Lady Llanover was known for her efforts to promote the Welsh language, traditions, and folk music during the 19th century.

PLACES:

Pontcysyllte Aqueduct: An engineering marvel, the Pontcysyllte Aqueduct in Wrexham, designed by Thomas Telford, is a UNESCO World Heritage Site and a testament to industrial-era ingenuity.

Big Pit National Coal Museum: Located in Blaenavon, this museum provides insights into the coal mining industry, reflecting the industrial heritage of Wales during the 19th century.

EVENTS:

Industrial Revolution: The 19th century witnessed the peak of the Industrial Revolution in Wales, with significant developments in coal mining, iron and steel production, and other industries. This era brought about urbanisation and social transformations.

Rebecca Riots (1839-1843): A series of protests and disturbances, known as the Rebecca Riots, took place in rural Wales, primarily against toll gates and perceived economic injustices.

Disestablishment of the Church in Wales (1914): While the disestablishment occurred slightly after the specified timeframe, it had its roots in the late 19th century. The Church in Wales was officially disestablished from the Church of England in 1914.

1901 – 2000

The turbulent 20th century saw Wales navigating the challenges of two World Wars, economic shifts, and political changes. The establishment of the Senedd in 1999 marked a significant step towards devolution and self-governance.

WELSH CONTRIBUTIONS AND IMPACT ON THE ECONOMY

Within the bounds Welsh history, the times encompassing the tumultuous chapters of World Wars I and II unfolds as a magnum opus, transcending the confines of historical records to become a dark era across the undulating landscapes of hills and valleys. This period intertwines vibrant hues of sacrifice, industrial metamorphosis, and societal tenacity, leaving an indelible mark on the collective consciousness.

As the world plunged into the abyss of the First World War in 1914, Wales, a microcosm reflecting broader geopolitical dynamics, stood at a poignant crossroads. The response of Welsh men, propelled by an unwavering sense of duty, reverberates through the corridors of history. The Battle of Mametz Wood, a poignant movement, etches an unforgettable chapter. The 38th (Welsh) Division, entrenched in the sombre theatre of the Western Front, contributed valiantly, imprinting their courage onto the very soul of the land they defended. David Lloyd George, a towering figure in British political history, holds particular significance for Wales, as he not only ascended to the position of Prime Minister but also championed the causes of his Welsh roots. Born in Manchester in 1863, Lloyd George's political journey began as the Member of Parliament for Caernarfon in 1890, representing a constituency deeply connected to Welsh heritage.

DAVID LLOYD GEORGE

Lloyd George's leadership during World War I marked a crucial chapter in the history of Wales. As the wartime Prime Minister, he guided the nation through tumultuous years, making decisions that echoed across the serene landscapes of his homeland. His role in coordinating war efforts and implementing reforms had a direct impact on the people of Wales, and the hills bore silent witness to the sacrifices made by Welsh communities.

Beyond the war, Lloyd George continued to champion the interests in Wales. His advocacy for social reforms, including efforts to address issues like housing and education, resonated with the needs of Welsh communities. Moreover, his role in the Paris Peace Conference of 1919, where the post-war order was negotiated, highlighted Wales on the international stage.

Lloyd George's legacy in Wales is not merely political; it encompasses a commitment to social justice and the well-being of his fellow countrymen. The hills of Wales, now transformed but still holding firm grip of the past, whisper tales not only of the sacrifices made during war but also of a statesman who, through leadership and vision, left an indelible mark on the history and identity of Wales.

Simultaneously, on the industrial front, the coalfields of South Wales underwent a transition, evolving into a pulsating heart responding to the exigencies of war. The mines, once symbolic of daily toil, assumed a heightened urgency. Coal, transcending its utilitarian role, emerged as a lifeline for the war effort, a testament to the industrial prowess etched into the nation's very essence. Visionaries like Aneurin Bevan, who would later become a prominent political figure, navigated the intricate challenges of wartime industrial production, leaving an indelible imprint on wartime accounts in Wales.

Throughout World War I, the hardworking women of Wales played a pivotal role on the domestic front, making substantial contributions to the war endeavour. As a considerable number of men enlisted in the armed forces, women stepped into various sectors, including the demanding coal mines. These determined women assumed challenging roles traditionally held by men, ensuring a consistent supply of coal critical for the nation's energy requirements and wartime machinery. Their commitment and diligence in the mines not only supported the war effort but also challenged conventional gender norms, setting the stage for a more inclusive workforce in the subsequent years.

The resolute spirit demonstrated by Welsh women during this era illustrates their tenacity and resolve in the face of challenging circumstances.

INDUSTRIOUS WELSH WOMEN DURING WORLD WAR I

The interwar interlude, marked by economic strife, cast a sombre pall over Welsh communities. The post-World War I decline in coal demand reverberated through the valleys, leaving behind a landscape scarred by unemployment and economic hardships. However, amidst this melancholy, communities displayed a resilience akin to a rising crescendo. The hillsides, erstwhile silent witnesses to the rhythms of mining, echoed with the determined footsteps of communities diversifying their economic repertoire.

Evan Roberts, a respected Welsh preacher, holds a central role in the story of Wales, not just as a source of spiritual inspiration but also as a key player in steering economic rejuvenation amidst difficult times. Born in 1878 in Loughor, South Wales, Roberts became a prominent figure during the Welsh Revival of 1904-1905, a spiritual awakening that profoundly impacted the nation.

Beyond his pulpit leadership, Roberts' importance for Wales extended to the economic realm. The Welsh Revival, under his guidance, sparked a deep spiritual renewal, drawing people from diverse backgrounds to congregations and fostering a sense of community and moral responsibility. This spiritual resilience became a cornerstone for individuals and communities navigating the challenges of the era.

Moreover, Evan Roberts' influence reached into the economic landscape. The revival instilled a sense of purpose and unity that transcended religious boundaries, shaping social attitudes and motivating individuals to actively contribute to their communities. Roberts actively advocated for ethical business conduct, emphasising principles of honesty and fairness in economic dealings.

Amid economic difficulties, Evan Roberts emerged as a source of optimism, guiding Wales towards resilience and regeneration. His teachings instilled values that went beyond the spiritual domain, encouraging a renewed focus on community, integrity, and cooperative efforts. Rooted in the revival, this ethos played a vital role in shaping the economic environment by promoting a sense of responsibility and a commitment to principled business practices.

Evan Roberts, through his preaching and the far-reaching effects of the Welsh Revival, added another dimension to the story of Wales – one marked by resilience and rebirth not only in the spiritual sphere but also in economic aspects. His influence left a lasting imprint, shaping the character and values of Wales during a challenging period in its history.

EVAN ROBERTS, THE REVERED WELSH PREACHER

WALES THROUGH THE TIMES OF WORLD WAR II

World War II, an era of unparalleled significance in the books of history and thrust Wales once more into the global spotlight. The rhythm of industrial prowess emanated from factories and shipyards, entwined with the haunting echoes of wartime sirens. The harrowing Swansea Blitz of 1941 unfolded a vivid tableau of destruction, leaving indelible scars on the very fabric of landscapes and communities.

Remarkably, the steadfast courage and unwavering resilience exhibited by the resilient citizens of Cardiff stand as an enduring testament to the human spirit, especially during the harrowing events of the infamous "Three Nights' Blitz" in January 1941. In the face of relentless adversity, the people of Cardiff forged a collective resilience that reverberated through the narrow streets and wide-open spaces alike. Families sought refuge in makeshift shelters, their homes reduced to rubble, yet their indomitable spirit remained unbroken.

The haunting wail of air raid sirens punctuated the cold night air, signalling the impending danger that would soon unfold. As the city endured wave after wave of devastating bombings, its skyline transformed into a fiery tableau of destruction. Through the darkness, the citizens emerged as beacons of hope, demonstrating a unity that transcended the physical and emotional toll exacted upon them.

The streets, once bustling with life, now bore the scars of war, yet they also bore witness to acts of compassion and solidarity. Neighbours supported each other amidst the chaos, sharing whatever resources they could muster. In the midst of destruction, a sense of community flourished, forming an unspoken bond that bound the people of Cardiff together.

THE BLITZ IN CARDIFF (1941)

The aftermath of those tumultuous nights saw a city rebuilding not only its structures but also its collective spirit. The resilience displayed during those sombre wartime echoes through the years, a poignant reminder of the strength that emerges when communities unite in the face of adversity.

In the midst of the tumultuous era of World War II, Aneurin Bevan stood out as a stalwart figure whose influence would leave an enduring mark on the social landscape of Wales. Born in Tredegar in 1897, Bevan emerged as a guiding force during a time when profound societal changes were afoot.

Aneurin Bevan's significance lies prominently in his role as the architect of the National Health Service (NHS). As a Labour Member of Parliament and Minister of Health in Clement Attlee's post-war government, Bevan spearheaded the establishment of the NHS in 1948. This groundbreaking initiative aimed to provide healthcare services to all citizens, irrespective of their socio-economic status. In Wales, a region historically marked by economic challenges, Bevan's vision for universal healthcare resonated deeply, making a substantial impact on the well-being of the Welsh population.

Bevan's commitment to social justice and his unwavering belief in the power of collective responsibility were instrumental in the creation of the NHS. His legacy endures in the hearts of the Welsh people, as the NHS became a symbol of equitable access to healthcare, embodying the principles of solidarity and compassion.

Beyond his role in healthcare reform, Bevan was a vocal advocate for the rights of workers and a champion of social equality. His influence in reshaping the social fabric of Wales during this period extended to issues such as housing and education. The Labour government's commitment to building a fairer society resonated strongly in Wales, where industrial towns and communities faced considerable challenges.

In the context of World War II, women assumed a central and empowering role in the Welsh workforce, contributing significantly to the wartime resilience of the nation. The collective Welsh society, once muffled by the cacophony of conflict, pulsated with newfound unity and shared purpose under the visionary leadership of figures like Aneurin Bevan. His legacy remains integral to the identity of Wales, representing a transformative period marked by social reforms and a commitment to the well-being of its citizens.

The post-war era, marked a resounding crescendo of change for Wales. Traditional industrial notes, embodied by the coal mining industry, gradually subsided, making way for a transformative movement. As mentioned, the establishment of the NHS in 1948, an intricate composition of social welfare, emerged as a beacon of light in the aftermath of the war's dark days. The echoes of wartime sacrifice became intrinsic threads woven into a society that emerged from the tempest stronger, more united, and adorned with the blossoming of progress.

ANEURIN BEVAN

The times of World Wars I and II intricately wove itself into the rich fabric of Wales, with each movement marked by poignant events. The valiant deeds of Welsh soldiers, the industrial progress during wartime, the adaptiveness in the post-war era, and the indomitable spirit demonstrated during the "Three Nights' Blitz" collectively defined the trajectory of the nation. Each meticulously etched movement.

WALES FROM POST-WAR RECONSTRUCTION TO DEVOLUTION

Following the culmination of World War II, a substantial stride was aimed at fostering the well-being of communities across Wales. Additionally, industries integral to economic fabric in Wales, such as coal mining, underwent nationalisation during this era, symbolising a crucial juncture in the nation's economic position.

In the ensuing decades, Wales confronted the formidable challenges posed by deindustrialisation, particularly in time-honoured sectors like coal and steel. Communities once reliant on these industrial strongholds found themselves grappling with economic tribulations. This transformative shift prompted an imperative need for economic diversification, compelling an exploration into uncharted sectors to cultivate resilience in the face of evolving economic landscapes.

The post-war era bore witness to a cultural renaissance and the rekindling of a fervent national identity. A watershed moment transpired in 1967 with the enactment of the Welsh Language Act, a legislative triumph that not only recognised but ardently protected the Welsh language. This cultural revival manifested as a flourishing pride in Welsh heritage and traditions, breathing new life into the now well-established Welsh identity.

The 1967 Welsh Language Act, referred to as Deddf Yr Iaith Gymraeg 1967 in Welsh, was enacted by the UK Parliament. This law granted specific rights for using the Welsh language in legal proceedings in Wales, including Monmouthshire. It authorised the relevant minister to approve the creation of Welsh versions of documents required or permitted by the Act. The legislation also repealed a section of the 1746 Wales and Berwick Act, which previously defined Wales as part of England.

WELSH LANGUAGE ACT (1976)

Passed in July 1967, this act was influenced by the 1965 Hughes Parry Report and advocacy from the Welsh Language Society and members of Plaid Cymru. Despite its enactment, some campaigners argued that the legislation fell short of their expectations. Notably, the Welsh Language Act marked the initial significant improvement in the rights to use Welsh in legal proceedings, signalling the start of overturning the historical ban on the language in law courts and public administration, which had been in place since the 16th century in favour of English.

A historic juncture materialised in 1997 with the devolution of powers to the nascent Welsh Assembly. This marked a decisive shift towards self-governance, affording Wales greater autonomy over its affairs. The establishment of the Welsh Assembly stands as an indelible milestone, profoundly influencing and shaping the political landscape of Wales.

THE MINERS' STRIKE OF 1984-1985 AND ITS IMPACT ON WALES

The politically charged period spanning the 1980s and early 1990s in Wales was marked by fervent political and social activism, with one of its defining moments being the Miners' Strike of 1984-1985. This resolute response from the mining communities was prompted by the government's plans to close numerous coal mines, a move that threatened the very foundation of these communities and their traditional way of life.

At the heart of this tumultuous period were key figures whose actions and decisions played a pivotal role in shaping the socio-political landscape. Arthur Scargill, the leader of the National Union of Mineworkers (NUM), emerged as a central figure in mobilising the miners against the proposed closures. His charismatic leadership and unwavering commitment to the cause galvanised the mining communities, turning the strike into a symbol of resistance against perceived injustices.

On the governmental side, Prime Minister Margaret Thatcher stood firm in her resolve to confront the powerful mining unions and implement sweeping changes in the coal industry. The clash between the formidable force of the government and the solidarity-forged miners created a tense and polarised atmosphere across Wales. Thatcher's firm stance on breaking the power of the unions and implementing market-oriented reforms intensified the animosity between the government and the mining communities.

THE MINERS' STRIKE LED BY ARTHUR SCARGILL

The Miners' Strike was not merely an industrial dispute; it became a broader socio-political movement that transcended the confines of the mining industry. Solidarity among miners and their families was unwavering, creating a powerful sense of community and shared purpose. Support for the striking miners extended beyond Wales, with other trade unions, sympathisers, and activists joining in solidarity protests across the UK.

The strike had profound effects on Welsh society, leaving an indelible imprint on the collective memory of the nation. The communities directly affected by the closures experienced economic hardships and social dislocation. The strike's aftermath witnessed the decline of the coal industry in Wales, leading to long-term repercussions for the affected regions.

The Miners' Strike was a watershed moment in Welsh history, encapsulating the intense political and social dynamics of the time. The clash between the mining communities and the government, not only symbolised resistance and solidarity but also left a lasting legacy on the socio-political fabric of Wales.

The denouement of the Cold War and the collapse of the Soviet Union in 1991 held ramifications of global import. While not directly impacting Wales, these seismic events exerted an indirect influence on the geopolitical landscape, shaping the broader global context within which Wales navigated its own transformative journey.

The period spanning from 1945 to 1999 encapsulated a dynamic and transformative time for Wales. The undulating currents of economic shifts, cultural resurgences, and political metamorphoses, entwined with the involvement of illustrious figures and the occurrence of pivotal events of modern Welsh identity within the intricate makeup of the United Kingdom.

ESTABLISHMENT OF THE SENEDD (WELSH PARLIAMENT) IN CARDIFF

In the intricate fabric of Welsh history, the year 1999 emerges as a profoundly significant period marked by the inception of the Senedd, the distinguished Welsh Parliament, nestled in Cardiff's core. This pivotal moment represents a substantial step towards devolution, endowing Wales with an enhanced degree of self-governance within the United Kingdom.

WELSH PARLIAMENT (SENEDD) FORMED IN 1999

The origin of this transformative phase can be traced back to the latter part of the 20th century, an episode when the political landscape of the United Kingdom underwent a transformative shift. The resounding call for devolved governance in Wales gathered unstoppable momentum, echoing the passionate aspirations of a nation eager to assert its unique identity and assume greater control over its internal matters.

The path leading to the establishment of the Senedd was no mere procedural formality; rather, it unfolded as an elaborate ballet of negotiations and contemplations spanning several years. Ultimately, in 1997, the height of anticipation was reached with a resounding 'Yes' vote in the Welsh devolution referendum. This momentous occurrence underscored the unequivocal popular mandate for the creation of a Welsh Parliament.

The realisation of this mandate unfolded grandiosely on May 12, 1999, as the inaugural session of the Senedd took centre stage within the resplendent Senedd building situated along Cardiff Bay. This historic event not only served as a physical hub for political discourse but also emerged as a symbol of the journey Wales faced towards self-determination. Within the venerable chambers of the Senedd, the resonance of democratic voices reverberated, crafting policies as intricate as the patterns of a tailor-made Welsh population.

Rhodri Morgan, a notable political figure in modern Welsh history, played a pivotal role in the era following the establishment of devolution and the Senedd. Born in 1939, Morgan became the inaugural First Minister of Wales in 1999 when devolution granted the Welsh government increased responsibilities. His significance lies in his contributions to shaping Welsh governance and policies during this transformative period.

Rhodri Morgan's political journey was marked by a deep commitment to Welsh interests. As the leader of the Welsh Labour Party and subsequently the First Minister, he advocated for policies that addressed the specific needs and nuances of Welsh society. His leadership style was characterised by pragmatism, a keen understanding of Welsh issues, and a commitment to devolved governance.

One of the key aspects of Rhodri Morgan's legacy is his role in establishing a distinctive Welsh approach to devolved matters such as education, health, and transportation. With the increased legislative competence granted to the Senedd, Wales gained the authority to make autonomous decisions tailored to the unique cadences of Welsh life. Under Morgan's leadership, the Welsh government focused on issues that directly impacted the people of Wales, working to improve public services and promote economic development.

RHODRI MORGAN (LEFT)

Morgan's tenure saw the consolidation and maturation of devolution in Wales. His approach emphasised collaboration and cooperation, seeking to build a stronger and more self-determined nation. His influence extended beyond political circles, making him a respected and influential figure in Welsh public life.

Rhodri Morgan's legacy endures in Wales, reflecting a crucial chapter in its modern history. His contributions to devolved governance, commitment to Welsh interests, and pragmatic leadership style have left an indelible mark. In the analogy of a proficient organiser guiding teams through masterful authority,

Rhodri Morgan stands as a statesman who skillfully steered Wales through the complexities of devolution, leaving a lasting impact on the nation's trajectory in modern times.

The establishment of the Senedd in 1999 is not merely a historical footnote but an illustrious chapter in the chronicles of Wales. With influential figures shaping the landscape, including the likes of Alun Michael and subsequent leaders, it symbolises not only a political watershed but also stands as a testament to the indomitable spirit of a nation shaping its destiny. The echoes of that momentous day persist, contributing to an ongoing story for Wales within the confines of the United Kingdom.

SUMMARY

In the 20th century Wales experienced transformative developments that influenced its social, economic, and cultural fabric. The era commenced with the Edwardian period, characterised by ongoing industrialization and the impact of World War I. The interwar years brought economic challenges, culminating in the Great Depression, while World War II ushered in significant disruptions and societal changes. Post-war reconstruction, coupled with the establishment of the National Health Service and educational reforms, contributed to social progress. The latter part of the century witnessed economic transformations, marked by the decline of heavy industries and subsequent efforts towards diversification. The 20th century in Wales was defined by a nuanced interplay of industrial legacy, global conflicts, social advancements, and economic adaptations, shaping the contemporary identity of the region.

PEOPLE:

Aneurin Bevan: A Welsh politician and one of the founders of the National Health Service (NHS) in the United Kingdom. Bevan served as Minister of Health and played a crucial role in shaping the post-war welfare state.

Dylan Thomas: A renowned Welsh poet and writer, Dylan Thomas is celebrated for his evocative and lyrical works, including "Under Milk Wood" and "Do not go gentle into that good night."

Rhodri Morgan: First Minister of Wales, who played a pivotal role in shaping modern Welsh governance during the era of devolution, emphasising the unique needs of Welsh society.

PLACES:

Port Talbot Steelworks: One of the largest steel production facilities in the UK, Port Talbot Steelworks in South Wales has been a significant industrial site throughout the 20th century.

Snowdonia National Park: Established in 1951, Snowdonia National Park in North Wales is renowned for its stunning landscapes, including the highest peak in Wales, Mount Snowdon.

EVENTS:

Devolution in Wales (1999): The establishment of the Senedd (Welsh Parliament) in Cardiff marked a significant moment in Welsh political history, granting Wales a degree of self-governance.

Miners' Strikes (1984-1985): A series of strikes by coal miners, particularly in South Wales, in response to proposed pit closures. The strikes had a profound impact on the mining communities and the broader labour movement.

Investiture of Prince Charles (1969): The investiture of Prince Charles as the Prince of Wales at Caernarfon Castle stirred both celebrations and protests, reflecting the complexities of the relationship between Wales and the British monarchy.

2000 – PRESENT

In the 21st century, Wales continues to evolve as a dynamic and culturally rich nation. Devolved government, economic diversification, and a vibrant cultural scene shape the contemporary Welsh experience.

FURTHER POWERS GRANTED TO THE SENEDD

In the chronicles of Welsh history in the 21st century, a notable period unfolds, characterised by the progression of devolution. This moment in time not only witnesses the strengthened position of the Senedd but also the amplification of its authority, signifying a profound evolution in the governance of Wales within the United Kingdom.

As the dawn of the new millennium approached, Wales stood on the brink of transformative change. The Senedd, having established itself as an emblem of Welsh autonomy, embarked on a journey towards greater empowerment. The pursuit of additional powers reflected steadfast commitment in Wales to shaping its own destiny, crafting an interpretation distinct from its counterparts in the United Kingdom.

The development of devolution during this era, with each legislative advancement contributing a distinct note to the composition of Welsh self-governance. The Senedd, housed within the architecturally splendid Senedd building in Cardiff Bay, became a focal point for political discourse, echoing the aspirations of the Welsh populace.

INSIDE THE SENEDD IN CARDIFF

The path towards increased powers was not without its complexities and debates. Discussions within the Senedd chambers mirrored the intricacies of formulating policies attuned to the nuanced needs of Welsh life. Notable leaders, once again figures such as Rhodri Morgan and Carwyn Jones, used the political landscape as a platform upon which they painted a vision of an empowered Wales. These leaders skillfully navigated the delicate balance between asserting national autonomy and fostering the collaborative spirit of the United Kingdom. Their contributions played a crucial role in shaping the trajectory of Welsh devolution in the 21st century.

The Wales Devolution referendum held on March 3, 2011, marked a pivotal moment in the evolution of governance in Wales, as it led to a decisive 'yes' vote, with 63.5% of the electorate supporting an expansion of legislative powers for the Senedd (Welsh Parliament). This referendum was a crucial step forward in the ongoing devolution process, solidifying the position as an individual nation capable of making independent decisions on a broader range of policy areas without seeking prior approval from the UK Parliament.

The outcome of the referendum granted the Senedd increased autonomy, allowing it to enact laws, or Acts, in key devolved policy areas, including education, health, and local government, without the need for Westminster's approval. This shift in constitutional dynamics represented a significant maturation of devolution, reinforcing the ability of Wales to shape its domestic affairs and policies according to its unique needs and aspirations.

With these enhanced legislative powers, the Senedd gained the capacity to craft policies that were more attuned to the specific nuances and preferences of the Welsh population. This move towards greater self-determination signified a deepening commitment to the principles of devolution, as Wales asserted its identity within the broader United Kingdom.

The Wales Devolution referendum of 2011, therefore, stands as a watershed moment in the devolutionary journey, underscoring the desire of the Welsh for increased autonomy and its evolving role in shaping its political and legislative landscape. This expansion of powers reflected not only a constitutional shift but also a manifestation of the Welsh people's aspiration for a more self-directed and responsive governance structure.

The strengthening of the Senedd's powers was not merely a legal formality; it symbolised maturation in Wales as a distinct political entity within the United Kingdom. The actions of the Senedd reverberated beyond its chambers, shaping the landscape of Welsh society and reinforcing a sense of national identity.

This era of devolution and heightened powers for the Senedd serves as a testament to the resilience and dynamism of the nation. It is a chapter enriched with the intricate strokes of political craftsmanship, embedded into Welsh history with a distinctly British flair. As the Senedd continued to thrive, its augmented powers resonating and drifting the spirit of a Wales confidently navigating its course in the ongoing story of the United Kingdom.

Covid-19 Strikes Wales

The impact of the COVID-19 pandemic on Wales has been profound, echoing the global challenges posed by the virus. Under the leadership of First Minister Mark Drakeford, the Welsh Government has navigated a complex landscape characterised by surges in confirmed cases, strains on healthcare resources, and disruptions to various aspects of society.

Wales, akin to the broader United Kingdom, has witnessed successive waves of COVID-19 cases and associated fatalities. The Welsh Government responded swiftly, implementing a series of public health measures. Lockdowns, social distancing mandates, mask requirements, and limitations on gatherings were enforced to mitigate the virus's spread and safeguard the populace.

In the healthcare sector, Welsh hospitals and dedicated healthcare professionals faced unprecedented challenges in managing the surge of COVID-19 patients. Initiatives were undertaken to augment hospital capacity, procure essential medical equipment, and roll out widespread testing to swiftly identify and isolate cases.

Responding to the crisis, the Welsh Government initiated an extensive vaccination campaign. This concerted effort aimed to achieve broad immunity and alleviate the severity of the disease. Vaccination centres were strategically established across Wales to administer vaccines to eligible populations in a phased approach.

Economically, the pandemic reverberated through various sectors in Wales, including hospitality, tourism, and small businesses. Lockdowns and restrictions posed challenges, prompting the Welsh Government to implement support measures to ease financial burdens on affected businesses and individuals.

The education sector underwent significant disruptions as schools in Wales grappled with closures and transitions to remote learning to curb the virus's spread. Likewise, many businesses embraced remote work arrangements to adhere to social distancing guidelines.

Throughout this challenging period, Welsh communities displayed resilience and solidarity. Local initiatives, support networks, and community-led efforts emerged to assist vulnerable individuals and those impacted by the crisis. This collective response underscored the strength of Welsh communities facing adversity.

As the situation continues to evolve, Wales, alongside the global community, adapts its strategies to address the ongoing challenges posed by COVID-19. The Welsh Government's focus on vaccination campaigns, sustained public health measures, and targeted economic support reflects an ongoing commitment to safeguarding the well-being of the Welsh population.

COVID-19 IN WALES

CHANGES IN INDUSTRY, TECHNOLOGY, AND CULTURAL IDENTITY IN CONTEMPORARY WALES

A profound tale now unfolds in Wales, detailing the intricate shifts in its economic, technological, and cultural landscapes. The evolution from an industrial powerhouse to a service-oriented paradigm reflects a nuanced response to the changing global context, depicting a story marked by resilience and adaptability.

Within the corridors of Welsh governance, a visionary journey into renewable energy is underway. This strategic venture, rooted in sustainability, marks a departure from traditional industrial norms. The ambitious commitment to achieving carbon neutrality by 2050 signifies a dedication to environmental responsibility. Wind, solar, and hydroelectric projects, reminiscent of architectural marvels, stand as symbols of the determination of Wales to forge a sustainable future, gradually moving away from reliance on fossil fuels.

THE RADYR WEIR HYDRO SCHEME

Technological prowess, akin to historical architectural marvels, is deeply embedded in contemporary Wales. The establishment of the National Cyber Security Academy in 2016 stands as a historical milestone, a sanctum where guardians of digital realms are nurtured. This institution reflects the commitment of Wales to fortifying cyber defences, a crucial chapter in technological evolution. Simultaneously, significant investments in digital infrastructure unfold as a civic project, reminiscent of historical efforts that connected diverse regions. This collective initiative aims to democratise high-speed internet access, ensuring every citizen participates in the unfolding episode of the digital age.

The cultural revival coursing through Wales evokes echoes from historical periods where cultural flourishing was a testament to societal vitality. The Welsh language, a living artifact, is diligently championed, echoing the preservationist spirit of ancient times. This linguistic rejuvenation, in schools and public life, mirrors historical valorisation of cultural identity. Similar to cultural renaissances of the past, a growing interest in Welsh music, literature, and art emerges—a special cultural regard across time.

Having being mentioned briefly in previous chapters, the National Eisteddfod is firmly rooted in Welsh tradition, historical festivities and crafting a vibrant tableau of artists cultural expression that spans through time.

Originating in the 12th century, the Eisteddfod is amongst the oldest cultural festivals in Europe, offering a stage for varied artistic expressions such as music, poetry, literature, and performing arts. Esteemed individuals, known as "eisteddfodwyr," converge to showcase their talents and engage in spirited competitions. The air resonates with the melodious strains of traditional Welsh music, the rhythmic recitations of poetry, and the dynamic performances that together form a proud cultural celebration.

A distinctive facet of the National Eisteddfod is the awarding of the Bardic Chair, an ancient tradition that crowns a bard for composing an exceptional piece of poetry on a given theme. This ceremonial event adds a touch of grandeur, underscoring the historical importance of the festival.

Importantly, the Eisteddfod serves as a link for influential figures and enthusiasts alike, fostering a sense of community and pride among those dedicated to preserving and promoting Welsh language and heritage. The festival is not merely a competition but a dynamic celebration where past and present entwine in a harmonious dance that reflects the enduring spirit of Wales.

Incorporating the presence of noteworthy individuals enhances the grandeur and significance of the National Eisteddfod, as it continues to be a vital chapter in cultural story of Wales.

EISTEDDFOD, AN INTEGRAL PART OF CULTURE IN WALES

The Welsh people, inheritors of a rich historical legacy, actively engage in preserving and perpetuating their heritage. Initiatives advocating the prominence of the Welsh language in education and public life echo historical campaigns for linguistic preservation. The flourishing of Welsh arts, supported by the government, finds historical parallels in the patronage of the arts by noble courts—a convergence of historical legacies and contemporary endeavours.

In the crucible of change, Wales emerges not as a passive observer but as an active architect of its destiny. The confluence of sustainable energy, technological prowess, and cultural revival paints a detailed historical scene—a tableau that resonates with the timeless reverberations of its storied past, while boldly inscribing new chapters into the historical scrolls of the 21st century.

SUMMARY

Into the 21st century Wales has continued to undergo notable transformations across various domains. The era is marked by advancements in technology, digitalisation, and a shift towards a knowledge-based economy. Devolution has empowered the Welsh government, allowing for increased autonomy in areas like health and education. Challenges such as economic disparities and the impact of global events, including the financial crisis and the ongoing complexities of Brexit, have shaped the socio-economic landscape. The preservation and promotion of Welsh language and culture remain significant focal points. Modern Wales is navigating a dynamic interplay of global influences, technological progress, and efforts to sustain its unique identity in the contemporary world.

PEOPLE:

Catherine Zeta-Jones: Acclaimed actress from Swansea.

Gareth Bale: Welsh footballer, known for his success with Real Madrid and the Welsh national team.

Rhys Ifans: Notable actor and producer hailing from Haverfordwest.

Laura Ashley: The Welsh fashion designer and businesswoman, known for her eponymous brand.

PLACES:

Cardiff Bay: The development of Cardiff Bay continued into the 21st century, transforming it into a vibrant waterfront area with cultural attractions, including the Wales Millennium Centre.

Millennium Stadium (now Principality Stadium): Hosting various sports events and concerts, the stadium in Cardiff underwent significant renovations, including the addition of a retractable roof.

EVENTS:

Wales Devolution (2011): A referendum in 2011 resulted in increased legislative powers for the Senedd (Welsh Parliament), marking another step in devolution.

Brexit: The United Kingdom's decision to leave the European Union in the 2016 referendum had implications for Wales, where there were varied opinions on the matter.

COVID-19 Pandemic: Like the rest of the world, Wales has been impacted by the COVID-19 pandemic, leading to changes in daily life, healthcare, and the economy.

Welsh Language: Efforts to promote and preserve the Welsh language continued, with initiatives in education, media, and cultural events.

Arts and Literature: Wales maintained a vibrant arts and literary scene, with authors and artists contributing to the cultural landscape.

The Eisteddfod: A venerable Welsh cultural festival that celebrates language, heritage, and artistic expression through competitions and performances, fostering a sense of community and pride.

Renewable Energy: Wales invested in renewable energy projects, including wind and solar power, contributing to efforts to address climate change.

Sports Success: Welsh sports teams, including the national football and rugby teams, experienced success on the international stage.

This list spans various fields and time periods, showcasing the diversity of influential individuals in the history of Wales.

LEGAL/POLITICS:

Hywel Dda (Hywel the Good) (880 – 950) - Ruler of Deheubarth and Gwynedd, known for codifying Welsh laws in the 10th century.

Gruffydd ap Llywelyn Fawr (1196 – 1244) - Ruler of Wales and key figure in Welsh history during the 13th century.

Dafydd ap Gruffydd (1238 – 1283) - Prince of Wales, brother of Llywelyn ap Gruffudd, and played a role in the struggles against English dominance.

Henry VII (1457 – 1509) - The first monarch of the Tudor dynasty, born in Pembroke Castle, instrumental in the Wars of the Roses, and became the King of England in 1485.

David Lloyd George (1863 – 1945) - The first and only Welshman to serve as the Prime Minister of the United Kingdom, played a crucial role in World War I.

Mark Drakeford (b. 1954) - Current First Minister of Wales, having taken office in December 2018.

MILITARY/POLITICAL:

Owain Glyndŵr (c. 1359 – c. 1415) - Led a rebellion against English rule, declared himself Prince of Wales, and remains a symbol of Welsh resistance.

Glyndŵr's Revolt (1400 – 1415) - Owain Glyndŵr's rebellion against English rule.

Lieutenant-General Sir Thomas Picton (1758–1815): Born in Haverfordwest, Pembrokeshire, Picton is often associated with Wales. He served in the British Army and fought in the Peninsular War under the Duke of Wellington.

Gwynfor Evans (1912 – 2005) - Founder of Plaid Cymru, the first Member of Parliament for the party, and a key figure in the Welsh nationalist movement.

Brigadier H. Jones, VC, OBE (1940–1982): David Jones, known as "H" Jones, was a British Army officer who posthumously received the Victoria Cross for his leadership during the Falklands War.

Major-General Sir Christopher Hughes (b. 1962): A contemporary military figure, Hughes has served in the British Army and held various command roles, including deployments to Iraq and Afghanistan.

LITERATURE:
Dafydd ap Gwilym (c. 1315 – c. 1350) - Renowned medieval Welsh poet, considered one of the greatest poets in the Welsh language.

William Morgan (1545 – 1604) - Translated the Bible into Welsh, contributing to the standardisation of the Welsh language.

Rhys Davies (1901–1978): A novelist and short story writer whose works often explored the lives of ordinary people in

Wales. Notable works include "The Withered Root" and "I Was Adored Once."

Gwyn Thomas (1913–1981): A novelist and academic known for his satirical and humorous works. Notable novels include "All Things Betray Thee" and "The World Cannot Hear You."

R. S. Thomas (1913–2000): A prominent Welsh poet and Anglican clergyman known for his exploration of Welsh identity and the human condition in his poetry.

Dylan Thomas (1914–1953): A celebrated poet and writer known for his vivid and innovative use of language. Notable works include "Under Milk Wood" and the poem "Do not go gentle into that good night."

Alun Lewis (1915–1944): A poet and writer known for his works reflecting his experiences as a soldier during World War II. His notable poems include "All Day It Has Rained."

Roald Dahl (1916–1990): Although born in Wales to Norwegian parents, Dahl spent his childhood in Wales. An internationally acclaimed children's author, his famous works include "Charlie and the Chocolate Factory" and "Matilda."

Gwyneth Lewis (b. December 4, 1959): A poet and writer who served as the inaugural National Poet of Wales. Her works include poetry collections like "Parables & Faxes" and the libretto for the opening of the 2012 London Olympics.

ACTING:

Richard Burton (1925 – 1984) - Acclaimed Welsh actor, known for his performances in films such as "Who's Afraid of Virginia Woolf?" and "Cleopatra."

Anthony Hopkins (b. 1937) - Academy Award-winning Welsh actor, acclaimed for performances in films such as "The Silence of the Lambs" and "The Remains of the Day."

Catherine Zeta-Jones (b. 1969) - Academy Award-winning Welsh actress, known for roles in films like "Chicago" and "The Mask of Zorro."

MUSIC:

Shirley Bassey (b. 1937) - Iconic Welsh singer, known for her powerful voice and international success with songs like "Goldfinger."

Tom Jones (b. 1940) - Internationally acclaimed Welsh singer known for hits like "It's Not Unusual" and "Delilah."

Mary Hopkin (b. 1950): A singer-songwriter from Pontardawe, Hopkin gained fame with her debut single "Those Were the Days" and represented the United Kingdom in the Eurovision Song Contest.

Bryn Terfel (b.1965): A renowned operatic bass-baritone, Terfel has achieved international acclaim for his performances in both classical and operatic repertoires.

Charlotte Church (b. 1986): A versatile singer and former child prodigy, Church has excelled in classical, pop, and contemporary genres, gaining international recognition.

SPORT:

Ian Woosnam (b. 1958): The Welsh golfer won the prestigious Masters Tournament in 1991, becoming the first Welshman to don the iconic Green Jacket.

Joe Calzaghe (b. 1972): Undefeated in his professional boxing career, Calzaghe held multiple world titles in two weight classes (super middleweight and light heavyweight) and retired with a perfect record.

Tanni Grey-Thompson (b. 1969): The decorated wheelchair racer won numerous gold medals at the Paralympic Games and set multiple world records during her illustrious career.

Geraint Thomas (b. 1986): The talented cyclist won the Tour de France in 2018, becoming the first Welshman to achieve this remarkable feat.

Gareth Bale (b. 1989) - Welsh professional footballer, known for his success with clubs like Tottenham Hotspur and Real Madrid, as well as the Wales national team.

Rugby Union (Team): Wales has achieved multiple Grand Slam victories in the Six Nations Championship, including notable years like 1908, 1909, 1911, 1950, 1971, 1976, 1978, 2005, and 2012.

Martin Miller-Yianni, born in 1958 in London, embarked on a career as a primary school classroom teacher, co-ordinating music. This followed his role as a dyslexia specialist, providing support to individuals with dyslexia across all age groups.

In 2005 in a courageous departure from the convention, Martin immersed himself in the adventure of venturing to Bulgaria. He assumed the roles of a journalist and researcher for a highly esteemed website dedicated to Eastern Europe while at the same time managing a smallholding in a village at weekends.

Martin swiftly gained profound insights into the diverse lifestyles and cultures of the area, spanning both urban and rural environments where he working and lived respectfully. His personal and professional connections across the region not only deepened his understanding but also provided fertile ground for his creative pursuits.

In 2020 Martin, faced life-changing health issues and his ability to work on his farm for the 'Good Life,' and engagement in sports and other physical activities ended. However, this setback opened up another door of opportunity in the realm of the creative arts. He now dedicates more of his time to writing, having now penned and published 15 books since 2020.

This exploration of different histories and cultures for books also stirred memories of the UK, particularly Wales, a place he fondly reminisces about. As a frequent visitor to Wales in the past, including an attempt at the Offa's Dyke path during his teenage years, and with his most influential music teacher being Welsh, to whom this book is dedicated, inspired the writing of another book.

INDEX

Image Caption	Image Source
The Royal Badge of Wales	Sodacan, via Wikimedia Commons
The Flag of Wales	flagcdn.com
The Location of Wales	David Liuzzo, via Wikimedia Commons
A Reconstructed Pre-Historic Semi-Permanent Camp	prehistoricarch.blogspot.com
Lligwy Burial Chamber, Moelfre, Anglesey	www.photographers_resource.co.uk
Moel-y-Gaer Hillfort in North Wales	Llywelyn2000, via Wikimedia Commons
Bronze Age Pottery Found in Cardiff	Vivian Paul Thomas, Cardiff University
Tre'r Ceiri Hillfort in North Wales	Llywelyn2000, via Wikimedia Commons
Castell Henllys Hillfort in Pembrokeshire	www.medievalheritage.eu
The Site in Segontium (Housed 100 Soldiers)	J. Thomas, geograph.org.uk
2nd Century Isca Augusta Roman Fortress	Public domain, via Wikimedia Commons
Sarn Helen Navigating the Undulating Welsh Terrain	John Lucas, via Wikimedia Commons
An Example of Roman Mosaic Found in Caerleon	Otter, via Wikimedia Commons
Roman General Flavius Stilicho	Public domain, via Wikimedia Commons
An Artist's Engraving of Dinas Emrys	National Library of Wales, via Wikimedia Commons
Vortigern and The Red and a White Dragons	Public domain, via Wikimedia Commons
King Offa Statue at Tintern Train Station	Colin Cheesman, via Wikimedia Commons
Map of The Offa's Dyke Route	Ariel196, via Wikimedia Commons
Chepstow Castle, Monmouthshire	Louis Haghe, Public domain, via Wikimedia Commons
Pembroke Castle, Pembrokeshire	JKMMX, via Wikimedia Commons
Gruffudd ap Cynan being freed from imprisonment by the Norman Lord Hugh d'Avranches in Chester	Thomas Prytherch, Public domain, via Wikimedia Commons
Llywelyn the Great	Rhion Pritchard, Public domain, via Wikimedia Commons
Llywelyn ap Gruffudd	Thomas Prytherch, via Wikimedia Commons
Battle-of-Mortimers-Cross (1461)	www.britishbattles.com
Henry VII Born in Pembroke Castle	Thomas Prytherch, Public domain, via Wikimedia Commons
Elizabeth I Brought Stability to Wales	Public domain, via Wikipedia
The Eve of the Battle of Edgehill (1642)	Walker Art Gallery, Public domain, via Wikimedia Commons
Act of Union with England in 1707	Public domain, via Wikimedia Commons
The Pontcysyllte Aqueduct	Steve Daniels, via Wikimedia Commons
Hub of Industry in Nant y Glo, Monmouthshire	National Library of Wales, Public domain, via Wikimedia Commons
Railway Station in Neyland, Wales	Public domain, via Wikimedia Commons
The Conwy Railway Bridge	Alfred Ashley, via Wikimedia Commons
Map of Coalfields in Wales (19th Century)	Public domain, via Wikimedia Commons
David Lloyd George	Unknown Photographer, Public domain, via Wikimedia Commons
Industrious Welsh Women During World War I	Public domain, via Wikimedia Commons
Evan Roberts, The Revered Welsh Preacher	Loughor Welsh Portrait Collection, Public domain, via Wikimedia Commons
The Blitz in Cardiff (1941)	Public domain, via Wikimedia Commons
Aneurin Bevan	Public domain, via Wikimedia Commons
Welsh Language Act (1976)	www.k_international.com
The Miners' Strike Led by Arthur Scargill	www.aworldtowin.net
Welsh Parliament (Senedd) Formed in 1999	Seth Whales, via Wikimedia Commons
Rhodri Morgan	Wales Office, via Wikimedia Commons
Inside the Senedd in Cardiff	www.cardiffbay.co.uk
COVID-19 in Wales	www.dailymail.co.uk
The Radyr Weir Hydro Scheme	renewablesfirst.co.uk
Eisteddfod, An Integral Part of Culture in Wales	RAY, via Wikimedia Commons

Serbia Through the Ages
(2023)
ISBN:
978-619-77423-7-4

26 Tales of Humanities Trials
(2023)
ISBN
978-619-92494-8-2

Simple Treasures in Bulgaria
(2008)
ISBN
978-0-9559-8490-7

I'm Bad at Poems
(2022)
ISBN
978-619-92494-2-0

Bulgaria Through the Ages
(2023)
ISBN
978-1-4476-2777-7

Redemption of Love
(2023)
ISBN
978-619-92494-0-6

100 Essential Recipes from Bulgaria
(2011)
ISBN
978-1-4477-0260-3

Romania Through the Ages
(2023)
ISBN
978-619-7742-19-0

North Macedonia Through the Ages
(2023)
ISBN
978-619-7742-25-1

Cyprus Through the Ages
(2023)
ISBN
978-619-7742-22-0